Captains Blog –

The Chronicles of My Afghan Vacation

ISBN 978-0-6151-6909-5

Published By Mark Bromwich / Lulu Press

Cedar Falls, Iowa 50613 ·

All photographs are provided by Mark Bromwich with the
exception of six which were provided by LCDR Less, and
Tracy you know which ones.

Special thanks to the members of the 554 QM BN Forward for
Allowing me the opportunity to spend the time with you, and being
able to tell some of your story as well. It is pretty common knowledge,
I am surprised you didn't know that.

Preface

This is the chronicles of a soldier who was deployed to Afghanistan to be an embedded trainer for the Afghan National Army.

Before the deployment I had been in the Iowa National Guard for a little over seventeen years, and had never before been deployed. Came close a couple of times, but never got asked to the big dance. Now it was that time, and I was excited about the prospect of getting to experience what so many soldiers before me had done.

During the preparations for the deployment I tried to think of a way I could keep in touch with everyone at home, especially my family and friends, without having to individually write, or email, each and everyone. Not that I wouldn't have done that, but if there was something out there that could simplify the process, I was all over it. It seemed like an awful lot of time would be devoted to trying to maintain contact, and not knowing what the environment would be like, I thought that maybe a blog would be the answer. I had never been much of a fan of blogging before the deployment, but now in retrospect, it was the best plan I could have thought of.

In the beginning the writing was plain, and I didn't really elaborate on a lot of anything to tell you the truth. Then as deployed life began to unfold in front of me, I found out that there was so much more to it, there was a story here. There was so much more to the war there than what was being portrayed in the media, and I wanted to tell that story, and I tried to tell it as genuinely as I possibly could. You may also notice that story is lacking in anything warlike, not because those experiences are absent from my memories, but simply because you can get plenty of that stuff elsewhere.

It is my hope as you read these postings that you get a sense of what it was like going through the deployment process, and what it is some of the soldiers from the US Military are actually doing over there. I also desire that you get a sense of what is Afghanistan, to include some experiences with the people, culture, and beliefs that make up this amazing country. Enjoy.

Here's the Start of Our Journey

Welcome to my Blog. I am not a huge fan of blogging, but I thought this would be the best way for everyone to find out how things are going while I am on this journey. I am quite privileged to have so many family and friends who are concerned about my well being, and I am certainly flattered by the support that I have received thus far. I look forward to the challenges I face in the future, and then sharing these challenges with you. Please feel free to post whenever you want, so I can stay in touch with what's going on in your worlds. I look forward to the exchanges we will have in the future. Once again, thank you and best wishes.

Sincerely,
Mark

Thanks for the Memories

I want to first thank everyone who made my going away party something to truly remember, at least the parts that I can remember. I really enjoyed seeing everyone there, and sharing the time together talking, laughing, and carrying on. It was very surreal for me, almost like being at my own wake. I know that sounds morbid, but if I was going to have a funeral for myself that I could attend, I would want to be just like that… simply awesome.

Here's an update on what's going on so far with my first couple weeks of Army stuff. We have been spending our time learning as much about Afghanistan's landscape, history and people as possible. It truly is an interesting country with a long and proud history. If you ever have the spare time you should Google it. The more I learn about the country, the more I look forward to getting there and becoming immersed into the culture.

Here's the downside, as many of you already know; we have been spending some time trying to learn some of the two major languages we are going to need to know. It is certainly not an easy task for myself, it's the old "old dog, new tricks" philosophy. So far with what I have learned, I do no think that I possess the skills required to order myself a sandwich. I think what would happen is that I would end up with trash can lid full of week old table scrapings that had been left in the sun. I'm working on it as best I can, I think by the time we are ready to come home I should be able to get my sandwich.

We've also been spending a lot of time mastering other military skills that will make the time spent in Afghanistan safer, such as weapons training and life saver skills. The life saver course we took part in required us to be able to successfully start an IV into a real human arm. I am thinking I'd rather spend time trying to learn Arabic than stick needles into another persons arm. I really didn't think I could do it, and I was sure my partner was having the same thoughts about my needle sticking skills. I decided to let my partner go first, and in this way he couldn't get "revenge" on me when I screwed up trying to get the needle into his arm. My partner did a great job getting the IV in, of course this made me even more nervous, and now I am thinking of a way to apologize for all the bruising his arm is going to experience when it was my turn to do the deed. Thankfully I was pleasantly surprised when I was able to get the IV in and going without him losing too much blood.

All in all; life is pretty good as far. The hard part comes next week, as we are moving onto our next stop on this journey … Mississippi. From what I have heard it's not the most pleasant place on the face of this earth, and I will certainly let you know when we get there. I wish you all well and thank you for the prayers.

Sincerely,
Mark

Wow ... What a Ride!!!

Hello All.   First thing I'd like to say is for all of you that were able to make that send off ceremony. I sincerely thank you. All along the way on this journey, the support from everyone has been fantastic, and I do appreciate it. It lets me know that what I am doing is appreciated.

Let me tell you about the ride to Mississippi, whew, what a ride. After our brilliant send-off we all loaded a bus, and started the eighteen hour trip to Mississippi. Our first driver was a little tired after a couple of hours on the road, and she started weaving all over the road. It made the ride a little more exciting to say the least. We talked her into pulling off to a truck stop to get some coffee to wake up a bit. After a few more nail biting hours we switched drivers, and things were pretty uneventful from that point on. After the bus ride we reached our destination of Mississippi, and excuse me for not telling you exactly where we are, as I really can't do that right now. If you know where I am at, keep that under your hat.

Now were at this army fort, and let me tell you hurricane Katrina was not very kind to this area. All along the road in Mississippi we saw houses and businesses destroyed by the hurricane. It was quite the downer to see the damage that was done to this state. The military place we are at was not excused from the damage either, and the place looks a bit depressing with all the damage that occurred. We moved right out to the field after receiving a cool briefing from the Colonel who will be our boss in Afghanistan. That puts us to where we are at now, which is I am on the Internet while sitting in my tent in the middle of Mississippi. Isn't technology grand? As our time here in Mississippi progresses I will keep you posted on all the interesting things I experience. Until then keep yourselves in good health and happiness.

Sincerely,
Mark

Mississippi Livin'

Hello all. Let's start off with some good news. We no longer live in a tent anymore, as we have moved into the barracks on you know where. We were supposed to stay a few days longer, but thanks to some prayer answered by Mother Nature, the days were cut short due to a huge storm moving in at us. You never realize how nice things like running water, mattresses, and porcelain toilets are. Seriously I feel bad for all the construction workers out there who have to use those Port-O-Johns on a regular basis. They suck …. And let me tell you when it sucks the most, about twelve noon in Mississippi as the sun hits the middle of the sky. Sitting in a Port-O-John with all your army gear on is no place to be, unless you want to loose five pounds in a flash, as they will turn into pile of melted human.

So, like I was saying, we are now in barracks. Our building is a long rectangular masonry brick building with rows of bunks beds down each side, and that's pretty much it. There is a row of windows towards the roofline on each side of the building, and a door at each end. Pretty sweet huh … trust me, after ten days in a tent it is heaven, and we are slowly but surely making it our temporary home.

We are continuing to train on army stuff everyday, and we continue to beat our bodies senseless with physical training. The army stuff we have been working on includes things like weapon systems, map reading, and leading troops. We spent one afternoon figuring out how to tell your direction using the sun and a stick talk about exciting, but in the middle of nowhere, it's all we had at the time and may come in handy some day. The beatings to our bodies include items like five to six mile road marches with about sixty to seventy extra pounds of army stuff (or shit as we call it) on. Once again in Mississippi during the day, well, let's just say that I go through a lot of uniforms due to fluid loss. The physical training isn't so bad really, I don't mind getting all tough again, although the road to getting tough is littered with a lot of sore muscles and blisters on my feet.

The coolest part of this deployment so far has been all the cool people I have met. The guys on my team all rock, and we all get along quite well. We all have our special talents and strengths, which really makes for a dynamic team that will be able to accomplish our mission and get home safely. Of course I got pegged as the e-mail / computer geek. If I only wore glasses and could get my hands on some tape, that would be awesome. As we live and work together we spend a lot of time working hard, and I tell you the thing that saves my sanity, is we all laugh a lot. I do not want to brag, as I am sure you all know, I am the one who gets the pot stirred up. Although; I've got a couple of my buddies here who give me a run for my money. I have also met a lot of other guys from all over the US, and they are all pretty cool also. The picture above is the Iowa team, my team. If you look closely at our faces, we have all started to grow mustaches, and we call it the stash club. We all look pretty sweet so far if you ask me, and I will certainly keep you updated on our progress. Everyone stay safe and healthy, and I will see you all soon. If you would like a mailing address for me/us, please send me an email, and I will reply with the address.

Sincerely,
Mark

enjoyed the experience of working with them. I pray that I never have to actually use the weapons during our mission.

Then we spent day training on hand to hand combat, which pretty much amounted to us pairing up and beating the hell out of each other. The Army brought in a team of professional trainers for this days event. The guys were specialists in martial arts and combat operations, so the training was excellent. I learned that I can be a can of whoop ass when you learn some simple techniques. The picture above is I and my partner Captain Eggers squaring off using rope as a weapon. As you can see by the way I am getting thrown down in a hurry, it works quite well. Eggers and I threw each other down about forty times each throughout the day, and it was exhausting after about six hours. If you look closely you can see that we are wearing the new "light weight" bullet proof army vests, and they weigh in about thirty five pounds or so. Getting up after each knock down took a while, as we felt like turtles stuck on our backs. After the day was done, there were a lot of sore muscles amongst the group, and people hitting the rack earlier than usual. It was actually one of the most enjoyable days we have had here, minus the big guns.

The climate in Mississippi is so interesting. One day it is blazing hot, and the very next day it can be a cold sixty degrees. It's crazy because you never know what to expect from one day to the next. Planning what to wear, besides the obvious it's going to be camouflaged, can be challenging at times. We haven't gotten any time off yet, so I have no idea what the area around this place is like, but we are hoping that Easter weekend we can got out and about to see what the area has to offer. I tell you though, the one thing that is never in question, and that is the power of hurricane Katrina. As we drive around this post getting to each of the training areas, we are constantly reminded of the damage that was caused by that storm. There are trees fallen all over and damaged buildings everywhere, it's simply amazing the damage that was caused by.

The last thing I wanted to note was Shelly and I had a close family member pass away this week. It was sad, as he was simply one of the coolest men I had ever met. He had a large heart of gold, and would have done anything for anyone in need. Uncle Jim is going to be missed greatly. I am saddened that I will miss the celebration of his life, and want to thank everyone who has landed their support to Shelly and her family while I am gone during trying times such as these.

Sincerely,
Mark

Road Rage Cured

Hello all and welcome back. Well we just spent the last five days working on convoy operations. A very useful skill set for Afghanistan, since we must move throughout the country via our Humvees, and for some reason the "bad guys" like to target our automobiles. I think it's a jealousy thing, as the Humvee is an awesome vehicle, and they can't have them. The more I drive a Humvee, and when I say drive I mean I drive it like a rental, the more I absolutely adore them. It has incredible power, is well balanced, and simply looks mean cruising down the road. Well in addition to driving the Humvee, which like I said before is awesome, then we add my second new favorite hobby, and that's firing the big guns, but now it's through the top of the automobile. For everyone who knows me, you all know I'm not really a "gun guy", but man there has to be something said for driving down the road at about thirty miles an hour. I'm standing out of the top of a hard-topped Humvee, dust and road grit burying itself in my face. I'm grasping the handles of a fifty caliber machine gun firing away at will into the tree line, making sure that no "enemies" decide we are their easy target. Now that's pretty sweet!!! The picture above says it all. Overall the training was excellent. Of course with everything good there has to be something "bad". Here's the bad part of the last five days. Our accommodations were less than stellar. We stayed in …

well to put it simply … in a gravel parking lot. When we live out in the field we usually live in built up bases called FOB's (Forward Operating Bases). Now these bases are usually equipped quite nicely with creature comforts such as electricity, dining halls, and shower structures. The parking lot had none of these amenities; in fact it didn't even have electricity, just two tents and a building without walls on the sides. Like I said it was a gravel parking lot, and decided to call it the FOPL (Forward Operating Parking Lot). It was one of those reminder things of how I take so many things for granted. Simple things like electricity and running water. When I

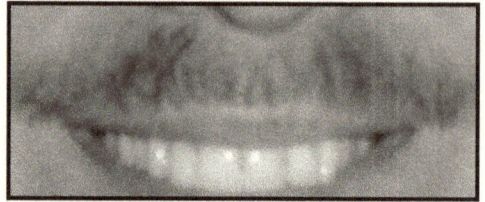

have to try and figure out how to live without them, it makes for challenging days. My favorite was trying to conserve my cell phone power to make sure we could call home though the whole exercise. From what I understand some of these conditions may exist when I get to my final destination, and so I guess it goes along with General Honerays' (I'm a can of whoop ass) plan, to immerse us in everything we may face in the future. Uncle Russ is really thinking these things through, and to think I thought he might have been a little on the madman side.

Stash Update: The stashes we're growing are looking quite nice as you can see in the picture. In fact mine is getting to the point where I'll have to do some trimming to meet the Army standards. Our big moustache move - when ever someone makes a profound statement, we all stop and rub our moustaches and mumble in agreement. It's pretty funny. We also all have agreed that our significant others may not agree with our stash growing, or they way the moustaches look on us, and so consequently when we return home from our leave no one will return with their moustaches. It's okay ... we'll just have to start over.

Sincerely,
Mark

PSA - I also want to put a shout out to all the taxpayers out there who paid their taxes that allowed us to get cool army gear such as the "Sleep System", which is a fancy army term for warm ass sleeping bag. A couple of nights out at the FOPL got kind of cold, and if it weren't for the sleep system we would have frozen our asses off.

Meet the Generals

Greetings from sunny Mississippi. Yesterday was a day to remember. We got notice a couple of days ago that we were going to have breakfast with some dignitaries, but we were unsure as to who it

was. When we arrived at the dinning hall to have breakfast, instantly I noticed that things were

quite unorganized, and I'm thinking that I wish I were still in bed. Things started to settle down, so we got into the line to get breakfast. This is where things started to get good. There were a couple of things that I didn't recognize right away. This first thing was plates and coffee mugs made out of ceramic; it was incredible, as since we have been here I have done nothing but eat and drink out of Styrofoam. The second thing I noticed was that the utensils were actually made of metal, real metal I tell you. Once again since we have been here I have eaten with nothing but plastic utensils. Really bad plastic ones, the kind made to frustrate humans because they bend and break easily. So now I am thinking this may turn out to be pretty cool. Then we find out who has called us to this wonderful meal. It is (two star) Major General Durbin, who just so happens to be the Senior Advisor to the Minister of Defense and the Army Chief of Staff in Afghanistan. He also brought with him (three star) Lieutenant

General Doory, who happens to be the Vice Chief of Staff of the Afghanistan Army. Now I am not one to name drop, but these guys are both pretty much some big shots in my world right now, and to think I had the privilege of having breakfast with them. Pretty sweet huh!!! In fact that happens to be the General with me in the photo above, just in case you were unsure. Both men spoke after our meal, and both speeches were really inspirational and informative. It was great when General Doory spoke because he really let us know how much he was thankful for what we were doing for his country, and he let us know about the progress that is being made to make Afghanistan a safe and free country.

Today we spent the day teaching, which was pretty sweet for me. I was longing for the opportunity to be in a classroom again, so it was nice to stand in front of a crowd again. Here's the twist though. The classroom I taught was supposed to be a room full of Afghani soldiers (my team members played the "students/soldiers"), and we had to teach our class through an interpreter. Not something I was used too at all, as it really changes the tempo and dynamics of the classroom. We had another interpreter in the audience as well, and he was to act as a student who we could ask questions of, or he could ask questions of me as well, both of course through my interpreter. It was pretty wild, but I had a good time, and did pretty well once I got used to the change in the classroom environment.

The next few days we are headed back out to the ranges to do some more shooting. Around here they are not afraid of putting a few rounds down range, as the bullets … they are a plenty thanks to "Uncle Russ."

Another thing that made me smile today is I bought my ticket to come home for leave. Man …that put a huge grin on my face; to know that I get to come home for a bit to see my family and friends. As it stands right now we are right about at the fifty days left point, and as the days pass I know I am closer to being home. Sometimes the wait to get home is brutal, and it seems like that day is never going to get here, especially the days when things here are not as pleasant. The one thing I always keep in the back of my mind is that the time I am away is short when I compare it to how much time I will have and have already spent with all of you, so I don't get to down about it. However; see you all soon, and stay healthy, happy, and safe.

Sincerely,
Mark

Time in a Bottle

Hello Everybody. I hope all is well at home in Iowa. Here in Mississippi things are pretty cool, minus the weather. As we move through the month of April the heat here is getting progressively warmer. It would be alright if we could cruise around here with shorts and a t-shirt, but the Army's got this whole uniform thing we have to adhere to. The other day we got all our new equipment for our deployment, pretty sweet looking stuff. We were issued things like body armor, backpacks, and other army type stuff. Well we put it all together and started wearing all this stuff for training, and it seemed awfully heavy, as today as I was walking past the fitness center I stopped in to weigh myself with all the new stuff on. I was shocked when I found out I had gained seventy pounds, no wonder my body hurts at the end of each training day. The good side of the new equipment is when ever I take the stuff off I feel like I am walking on air, and the extra weight is really helping trim down on my extra weight. The down side is I think I have shrunk an inch in height since we have started wearing it.

The beginning of the week was spent learning about urban operations. We trained on topics such as dealing with civilians on the battlefield and working together in close quarters operations. It was my favorite training so far since we have been here, because it was so realistic. The training site we used had a whole "village" constructed for us to train in, and then to add to the realism they had about fifty people dressed as civilians "living" in the village. We had to go through the village and negotiate obstacles such as sniper fire or extracting a suspected insurgent from a building without causing harm to the civilians. It was hard training, at the end of each day I was absolutely exhausted, but overall the experience was quite worth it.

After urban operations training we have spent the last couple of days working on basic soldiers skills. We went back to basic training for a while doing tasks such as low crawling, first aid, and gas mask training. This training was the same stuff we did in basic training, and as I was sitting in class learning some of the tasks again, it dawned on me that it had been eighteen years since I had been to basic training. The classic cliché dropped right into my lap, man does time fly by. I couldn't believe that I have been doing this stuff for over eighteen years already. Then after I got up from the low crawling exercise I realized, yup I have aged eighteen years, and my body doesn't quite tolerate this stuff like it used too. Then to top off the basic soldiers skills training we headed off to the gas chamber to get a mouthful of CS gas. Now when we do the gas chamber they use the guise that this "training" is to help us gain confidence in our protective masks. In saying this; sure that sounds like a fine justification for the chamber, but I have all been in the gas chamber a number of times, and let me tell you I am quite confident that my mask will work. However, I think my negotiations skills are slipping, because I ended up going in the darn thing anyways. It's not all that bad to tell you the truth. Once exposed to the gas you get all teary eyed and snot hangs out of your nose to about your knees. No worries though, the effect doesn't last all that long, and the gas is harmless with our very limited exposure. I don't want you guys at home to think they are putting us in harms way.

If you are curious about the picture above, it is me putting in an IV. I was practicing my combat life saving skills. We go through a five day course on how to be life savers, and basically the course is a very trimmed down version of a course an EMT might take. We learn how to put in IV's, nasal tubes, needles in the chest to aid a collapse lung (they don't let us practice the last one on real people). Since the class we all have been continuing to hone our skills, especially the IV's, to better prepare ourselves to help a buddy out in a time of need. The person you see there graciously volunteered to be my second successful IV into a real human. It's pretty awesome because I have been pretty successful in getting in the needle and catheter in the first time for each of my patients. Thankfully for them.

Well; as the days pass I am closer and closer to getting home for our leave, and I look forward to seeing as many of you as I can in the short time I will be home. More importantly once I return from leave I can get in a plane and get over there to start counting the days until I return home for good. That's the one hard thing about Mississippi, the time here doesn't seem real because I still have all the time to spend over there yet, and that clock hasn't even started ticking yet. Soon enough though. The one nice thing about Mississippi is that I am meeting more and more people here, and they are all pretty cool. I am definitely making some new lifelong friends though this experience, and that's awesome. So another cliché drops right into my lap, no matter where people are from and what backgrounds they have, when we all get together for a single cause, all that stuff doesn't seem to matter. We all want to get over there, do our jobs the best we can, and get home safe and around to our families. Talk to you all soon, and may your days be filled with health and happiness.

Sincerely,
Mark

Cheeseburgers in Paradise

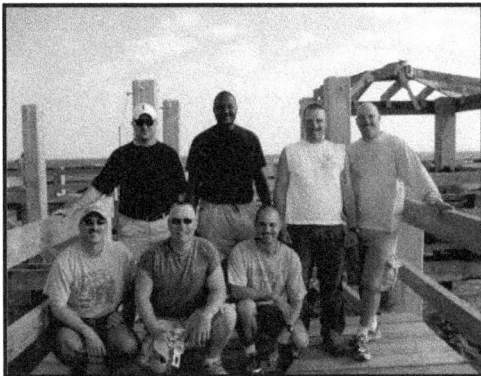

Greetings from Mississippi … It's great to be back here at the Gordon Lakes Club. This week was pretty quiet for me, as far as training is concerned. I spent last week (40 hours) learning about one of the new radios we will use over there. The course was pretty in depth on the programming and use of the radio, which was quite exciting for me, but I am sure the rest of you don't care all that much about my radio training, so lets move on to the next topic.

On Saturday we did a live fire exercise where the mission was to clear all of the "enemies" from a building, while making sure the "civilians" were left unharmed. The enemies and civilians come in the form of plastic silhouettes, and good guys are tan, while green ones are the bad guys. We clear the building using four man teams in what is called a "stack" formation. We had been practicing our four man stack room clearing techniques here and there with blanks for a couple of weeks now, so we were quite ready for the real thing. We called ourselves Team AARP, we decided on this because we were pretty sure together we had the highest combined age of all the teams. Right before we went in we were asking the sergeant who was our observer / safety if the rooms were handicap accessible, and if hearing protection meant that we needed to turn our hearing aids down. He thought we were all pretty entertaining. Underneath the jokes I was pretty stoked though, as I have never fired live bullets in this type of scenario before, so the adrenaline was flowing pretty heavily through this old mans veins. When you are firing live bullets in a house, and there are live bullets flying to right and left of you, it's pretty exciting. We had a great time, and as a team we performed quite well. And just so you all know, none of the plastic silhouettes were harmed in the making of this posting.

After Saturdays training was complete we received a pass for a little over twenty fours hours, and let me tell you what, I truly needed it. A group of us decided to rent cars and see some of what Mississippi had to offer. We got rooms at the local Holiday Inn, and commenced to consuming adult beverages. After a few of them we decided it was time to partake in the Hattiesburg nightlife. The first establishment we went into was a country bar across the street from the hotel. As soon as we stepped in it was like being in a movie. The bar was your stereotypical right out of the movie Roadhouse kind of place, so we didn't stay long. We then went to the next place, and to our amazement, another country bar. Once again we didn't stay long. We found another place called Ropers, and you wouldn't believe it if I told you, but yes, it too was a country bar. We decided to just stay there and enjoy all that Hattiesburg had to offer. I made an attempt at line dancing, and that didn't go all that well, so I decided I would just stick to my stool. Even though it was a country bar, not my favorite type of place, and my attempt at fitting in failed miserably, it was still better than being at back at the base. In fact overall I had a brilliant time.

The next morning after some Tylenol and a couple cups of coffee, the breakfast of champions, we decided we would take our cars and drive to the coast. Thinking it would be great to see the beach and frolic in the Gulf of Mexico, I really kind of forgot one of the most devastating storms in recorded history had just recently been there.

When we got there it was amazing, almost impossible to put into words the devastation the people who had lived there had to endure. It was simply unbelievable. In my estimation from the actual coastline to about a quarter of a mile inland was simply gone. All that was left were the signs of where businesses had been, and the foundations that once held them up. Any building that was over two stories tall would have the floors above that point damaged, but for the most part intact, and anything below that point everything was gone except for the skeletons of the buildings holding up the floors above.

Whole roads and bridges were up uprooted from the earth and tossed around mercilessly, then placed back down on into piles broken concrete. We spent the whole day driving, and walking when the cars could go no further, looking at the damage. It's going to take a long time to clean up the mess Mother Nature has made, and restore the city back into what it once was. When I thought about the all the people displaced, having lost everything they had, I tend to think my problems are not all that large anymore.

The day wasn't all bad though, maybe a little depressing at times, but we still had a brilliant time. We met some nice people, walked in the gulf, and even did a little crab fishing. Then we decided to have Easter dinner somewhere. It didn't take much decision making power to decide where it was we were going to eat. I had a cheeseburger and crab legs at the Gulfport Hooters restaurant. As their motto states … Delightfully Tacky, Yet Unrefined … is fitting.

I've rambled on now for more than enough, so I think I'll call this posting done. I once again wish you all safety and health. I also want to thank everyone who has posted, emailed, and sent mail to me. Things from home really make what would usually be unbearable far more tolerable, and I really appreciate it.

Sincerely,
Mark

Back to Basics

"Everything I needed to Know I learned in Kindergarten" Fulghum

Hello again all, I trust that this posting reaches you all in good health and spirits.

We have spent the last week or so learning how to drive, we went back to basic training, and we had some rainy fun. Read on …. You'll see what I mean.

When we get to our destination for the next year our primary mode of transportation will be the Humvee, which I am sure you have all seen before, but ours will have all kinds of armament to protect us. Brilliant idea, but it dramatically changes the way that the auto performs, so we spent time learning how to adjust to the changes. The new Humvee doesn't exactly drive like a new Cadillac by any means, but to tell you the truth I thought it actually drove better that the old ones by far. The ride seemed to be much smoother than your basic Humvee, and the vehicle handled well on all types of terrain. The best part is that the damn thing will stop bullets and explosions, totally worth owning. Did I also mention that the new Humvees also have air conditioning, that right I said AC. I'm thinking this is a much needed option, and look forward to having such creature comforts, next thing you know they'll come with stereos and electric seats. Then we get to the training and we find out that the AC tends to break a lot, and when we actually get our new Humvees that we should not look forward to having the AC. Oh well. I am unsure as to how long the warranty lasts, but still the options totally outweigh the lack of customer service, and can't wait to own one. While I was waiting to drive the new Humvee we got to drive what Camp Shelby calls "The Resister Course", which is basically a four wheelers dream drive. I got to put the Humvee through its paces, and really see what it can do. Let me tell you I drove it like a rental, I mean I beat the hell out it, driving over trees and hills. All through the drive I was giggling like a little school boy because usually we are not allowed to be so abusive. It

was an awesome course.

After the drivers training we spent the last four days in squad and platoon tactics. The training is very reminiscent to the stuff we all learned as young private's way back in basic training. For me basic training was about eighteen years ago, and for others on our team that date goes even further back. Our instructors for this block called it "infantry kindergarten", since it was such a return to what we all had learned so many years ago. I don't know about the rest of my team members, but I remember kindergarten being full of fun, with stuff like finger painting and Legos. The only thing that has changed from the early days is the amount of abuse my body can seem to tolerate. If I remember correctly this stuff didn't hurt as much back then as it did this time. Now maybe it's the extra seventy pounds of gear I'm carrying on my body, or maybe it was the oppressively hot weather, but every night when I returned to the barracks my body hurt. I'm not ready to admit to myself that maybe it's because I'm old, as that can't be the answer to why it hurts so much. Anyhoo, I don't mean to ramble on … let me tell you what we did. We started the four day session with individual tactical movements. We learned again how to low crawl, high crawl, and we even had to climb over a five foot wall to get through the IMT (individual movement techniques) course, it just like the stuff you see in the "war movies." Pretty sweet huh?? Then we moved onto squad tactics, getting used to moving in squad sized elements, and reacting to such challenges like ambushes or snipers. Finally we put the individual and squad techniques together to perform whole platoon tactics, reacting to the same scenarios, but in larger scale. The last day was spent planning and rehearsing for a deliberate attack. The mission was to attack a series of bunkers. By the time we were done taking out those bunkers, there wasn't much left of them. Kind of … since the whole thing was done in blanks we nominally destroyed them. Honestly damn it I'm old, and this infantry stuff is definitely for the young. To top it all off at the end of the last day it started to downpour, and I mean downpour. I don't know how much rain came down, but we were soaked. The amazing thing was that with the oppressive heat down here, the rain was quite welcomed, and we found ourselves actually enjoying getting wet. We even posed for a few pictures of us having fun in the rain.

Then when we returned to our barracks I noticed that between ours and the neighbors barracks there was a stream running between the two. What comes to mind …? Mudslides of course, so I and a couple of the other guys, to include our boss the colonel began to run and slide through the stream. We were already soaked, so it seemed like the right thing to do at the time. It was a nice release to what was a really tough four days. Well talk to you all again soon, and look forward to seeing as many of you as I can when I return in twenty seven days. I can't wait. Until then be good.

Sincerely,
Mark

Back to the City…The Tent City That Is

"I hear and I forget. I see and I remember. I do and I understand" Chinese *Proverb*

Salaam; Chetor Hastee, aayaa khudet naan khorda meytaanee.

First off, I better tell you all the bad news. I had a moustache mishap while trimming the 'ol soup strainer the other day. I accidentally lopped off just a hair too much (no pun intended), so I had to start all over from the beginning. Starting over was not such a big deal, but the when the stash club members noticed my naked lip, they gave me some crap about being a defector from the club and stuff like that. It was hard at first, being different from the others, but thankfully when the stash started to come back in I was allowed back into the club.

Well, enough of on that topic, as it hurts too much to dwell on it, and let me tell you what we have been up to the last eight days or so. To start things off we spent two days in an intensive language class. Maybe the language is too difficult, or maybe my brain is starting to gel because of old age, but the only thing I truly remember from the two days were the fantastic lunches I ate and how nicely the padding on the seats in the theater were. During one exercise the instructor had us do some writing exercises, and before we could go on break he wanted to check our work. The task was simple; write my first and last name in Dari. For most people no problems at all, they showed the instructor their work and he would make some small corrections, but for the most part he was quite pleased with their work. Then here comes my turn to show off my Dari writing talents. I proudly held my work up to the instructor, and he calmly asks me if I wrote my name in Chinese, and if I knew I had written "some bad things." It was at this point that I knew my career as a Dari translator was not going to become a reality, and that I am really going to need to take good care of my translator. Make sure that person is at my side at all times, and never write anything down without it being proofread first. Needless to say these two days turned out to be pretty long days for me.

After the language classes we moved out to the field, that's Army camping for my non-army friends, for a lovely six day / five night stay in a canvas tent. The mission was to train on base defense for the first three days, and then the last three days we were going to train

some "Afghanistan Army" troops on how to do what we had just learned. Here at Camp Shelby, Mississippi, they have painstaking built a whole Army base that mirrors what we may live in when we get overseas. Now I really dig realism for training, but I didn't need a reminder that while overseas the conditions may be less than adequate. Hell; my idea of roughing it is not having room service at the Holiday

Inn after ten o'clock, so living in a tent for the next six days was certainly not something I look forward too. You can see by the picture above that this is not like camping at your local state park. It's rows and rows of tents, and then the whole thing is wrapped with a protective barrier of guard towers, barbed wire, and some other stuff to keep people out. Pretty sweet!!!

Day one I spent my morning in class, and I was supposed to be learning how to defend our fine accommodations, but if you click this movie link, you will see that I wasn't as focused as maybe I should have been. After my short nap, off with my battle buddy I went to defend the base. We spent the rest of the day up in a guard tower, about twenty five feet in the air, waiting for the "enemy" to attack. Sadly the enemy never got to us, I think it's because I was too damn intimidating, but we spent our day looking out towards the woods, studying the traffic patterns of termites, and watching other get to defend to base from the bad guys.

Day two I learned how to defend the main entry way onto the camping site. The idea behind this task is to create a safe point for which the good guys can get onto the base, while keeping the bad guys out. We do this using a lot of firepower, blocking stuff all over the roads, and brilliant questioning techniques. I got to be the questing guy on the main gate, and let me tell you, no one got on my base without proper authorization. Those of you who know me can attest that I have a keen sense of wit mixed in with a small amount of sarcasm. It was this deadly mix that made me as successful as the "questioning guy" on the front gate. Not only was I able to separate the good from the bad guys, but I am pretty sure I keep our graders in stitches the entire day.

Day three started out in class again, and the topic of the day was how to protect the outside of the base, kind of like a state park warden. We drive around our base in our vehicles, and if there are bad guys getting uppity out there the walls, we would discourage them from getting in by using our powers of persuasion in the form of very large guns. My mission this day was to be a passenger, and keep my eyes peeled, so not a whole lot of excitement for myself. However, a pretty good day as a group we were able to keep our camping site safe.

Now the fun starts. The next three days every morning our team went to the operations center and received our mission. Each day was something different, like one day we had to rescue two workers that got lost in a dangerous area, or the next day we had to go out and analyze mortar craters to try and figure where they were fired from. Normally these missions are pretty easy on our own, but the difference is we had to let the Afghanistan Army troops do the work. Our job was to guide and mentor them on how to complete the tasks at hand, but really let them take ownership of the missions. The soldiers did it all, they planned, rehearsed, and the attempted to complete their plan. The group of soldiers we worked with had just returned from a deployment, and so for the most part were a pretty squared away group. However, I think they were instructed to be either the highly motivated group, or they could be the not so motivated group, to add a little bit of a challenge to the mentoring part of the mission. Depending on the group you received in the morning, you could have either a pretty easy time with the days work, or you could have a challenging time getting everything together to accomplish the tasks. I liked this twist, because that's they way it's going to be, not all my days in Afghanistan are going to be effortless with the troops I train. Overall we had a brilliant time, and it was great to be training in an environment that tried to reflect our mission.

As the time here gets short, I am definitely seeing the focus of our training shift from training us to be self sufficient cans of whoop-ass, which is pretty sweet, to now training us to be able to pass what we have learned over the last sixty days and our careers as soldiers onto the soldiers in our charge. It's nice to see the conclusion of this chapter so close, but as I ponder the end of Mississippi, I only have a short time to reflect because the next big challenge is on the next horizon. I am not going to even consider this yet; first I have a ten day block of leave to which I must attend to. I can't wait to see as many of you as I possibly can. I know there is a Guinness with my name on it, and plenty of good conversation with you guys to go with it. Only about two weeks till then ... See you then.

Baamaane khudaa,
Mark

All that I know I learned at Camp Shelby

"I'm leaving Camp Shelby Now … I've done all I can here" MWB

Well folks; Camp Shelby has come to an end, and let me tell you it's tough to hold back the tears as I think of leaving this place. It has been a

whirlwind of ups and downs, good times and bad times, and a whole lot of in-betweens. Simply put Camp Shelby has created in me one super can of whoop ass, and now I am prepared to head out on my mission. I do not believe that I will spend a whole lot of time looking back and reminiscing about Camp Shelby in particular, as it hasn't been my favorite place on the planet, but I will remember all the fine soldiers I have met here, especially the fifteen other Iowans who I have grown very close to. I look forward to the future with them, as we move forth to the challenge of helping the people of Afghanistan. Before I can do that though, I get to come home for a ten day stint, and spend time with my family and friends.

Let me tell you about the last set of events that have occurred here at lovely Camp Shelby since the last time we talked. We spent our last few days in the field at another FOB (Forward Operating Base), and this one went by the name of Black Horse. I am unsure as to the origin of the name, and I thought it to be quite original, but alas when we arrived it was no different than any other FOB we had spent time at. The middle is lined with tents for us to sleep in and operate out of. There was a building to eat chow, not of the highest level cuisine that I have experienced in my life, but none the less it was good enough to keep us going. There was a building that acted as a shower facility, and one evening I went in to take a shower. Just as I was all soaped up all the water quit running, as I stood there all soapy and naked, I notice that I am standing next to this Major who experiencing the same situation and we try to small talk. It just seems a bit odd to try and chat during such a discomfited time, so I look over at him and say "well …. This is a bit socially awkward." We laughed for a bit, and thankfully the water started back up. The water is stored in giant black plastic bags that sit on the ground, and the idea is that during the hot Mississippi days the sun will heat these bags up, and provide water that should be warm, and I stress the should part, because every night I went in for a shower the water was so cold that one could almost see the icicles form as the water dripped of my body.

Anyhoo; I digress…the idea behind us going to the field this time is to again prepare to train the Afghan National Army, and to replicate this environment the Mississippi National Guard decided to help by donating the time of several of their soldiers for us to train with. They were a good group of military police, and together we had a brilliant time training. My mission was to teach them how to shoot their individual weapons, the M16A2 rifle. The first phase of the training plan was the Pre-Marksmanship Training. This is where the soldiers learn all the techniques for good shooting. Items such a breathing, trigger squeeze, and sight pictures are all a parts of this training to prepare them to shoot live rounds on the range. What I did was rally our team of trainers, and we taught them each these techniques during the morning of the first day. During the afternoon the soldiers from Mississippi then got to use a laser shooting system called the Beam Hit. The laser sits in the barrel of their weapons, and they shoot at various laser receptor targets. A computer then can tally their scores to see how well the techniques are working for them.

The next day we spent running an actual live range. It was awesome, and it actually ran quite smoothly. I had our guys in the

tower calling out the commands, and a group of us stood on the firing line coaching the shooters and making sure everything was safe during the event. It was a finely tuned, well oiled, humming machine to see us all work together like that. We just had a lot of fun with the Mississippi National Guard; however they were not the best shooters in the world, and it some time to get everyone shooting well. Now one would think that military police men would be incredible shooters, but to their defense the military police usually carry hand guns, and are not accustom to shooting rifles so we didn't give them to hard a time.

To pass the rest of the time in the field I helped teach a class for the other guys who had a mission to teach the soldiers on Common Task Training, helped keep the communications equipment running, played a few practical jokes, and I watched a couple of movies. Overall a pretty good time was had by all in the field.

After getting out of the field I spent my time packing up most of our gear, as that stuff is going to leave before we do, and hopefully it will get there when we arrive. Then we spent the next day practicing for our graduation. It is a huge get together of all the big wigs, and they are all arriving to see what cans of whoop ass Camp Shelby has turned us into. There will be state Governors, Generals from all over and of course friends and family who are able to attend. Now they say that the whole ceremony is for us, but the entire time this ceremony is taking place we have to stand with our body armor and helmets on in the hot Mississippi sun. I'm thinking that maybe it's not totally for us. I'm thinking standing in the hot sun with all that stuff on isn't my idea of a good time at all. But as you can see there are some perks, here I am with a couple of Generals. The one on the right is from Iowa (Deputy Adjutant General), me in the middle, and the other is a Minnesota General. Not to name drop, but I have hung out with a lot of Generals so far as you have noticed. When I take the pictures most of them ask; "now who are you again?" For some reason or another I get the feeling they'll remember my name, as I am sure it is not everyday some captain just waltzes on up to them out of the blue and snaps a picture with them. I try to make this journey as fun a possible I guess.

Sincerely,
Mark

The Leave is Now Over

"Go To Your Happy Place"   Chubbs

> *Twenty years from now you will be more disappointed by the things that you didn't do than by the ones you did do. So throw off the bowlines. Sail away from the safe harbor. Catch the trade winds in your sails.*
>
> Mark Twain

Here we are again, back at Camp Shelby, but this time it is to pack and leave and wait for our turn to move on to the next portion of this deployment. I really disliked leaving home again, especially to return to this place. Saying goodbye to everyone for a second time proved to be a pretty tough task. To be honest ... quite depressing really. I do want to make sure that I thank everyone for making my valuable time at home really well spent. Being home that short time was awesome. As soon as I stepped off the plane and embraced my family, it seemed as if I hadn't been away at all. Thankfully the mind is a brilliant organ, it has the ability to adjust spans of time for us, and help us with devices such a memories. I also want to thank everyone who has lent a hand in anyway to me and my family while I was away, and while I continue to be away. It means so much to know that things will be cool while I am gone. I also want to make sure I send a special thank you to the Doyle family for being there, and for Matt to making the continuation of this Blog possible.

I do want to ensure everyone that I am totally prepared for the journey, not only from the expert tutelage that Camp Shelby has provided me, but also in some lessons that I learned while on my ten day leave. I'll explain, which I am sure you all knew was imminent, in three major Pearls of Wisdom.

① Peace With Ones Inner Self

I'm cool with the journey I am about to embark on, and look forward to helping the people of Afghanistan. The trip is filled with so many unpleasant things that could or might happen, and of course that possibility strikes a little apprehension in me. I would be worried about myself if I weren't afraid of such things, but I believe that I will handle such situations the best I can. Right now as I prepare to leave the comfort of American soil I have an inner tranquility with the state of affairs, and believe that the positives will certainly outweigh the negatives.

② Don't Look Behind

I have to forget all that I have learned here at Camp Shelby, although I am sure there are tidbits of data gained from here that may

prove useful in Afghanistan, I am convinced that the bulk of schema built here will not serve me whole lot over there. I endeavor to learn all I can about my new paradigm, and get the most out of it. Not only accomplish my mission, but also learn about the people, the culture, and religion. Really make this trip worth my while, but when I return home, I will also do my best to only bring home memories worth having.

③ The Family and Friends Plan

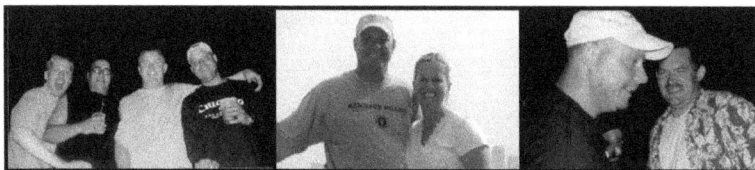

Going through this whole experience has taught me that family and friends are the most important assets I possess. I couldn't believe how much I missed these two key facets in my life while away. Now I have been away form home before, but for some reason this separation seems so much more different. It's tough to put my finger on the exact why, but I think it's purely time and place. Give me a year away form home, and when I return, I will have your answer.

Hopefully this post doesn't resound the babblings of a guy expounding on all things cliché. I just wanted to throw some things out there, so people can get a glimpse at the goings on in my mind before we hit the ground running. I know I don't openly discuss these things socially, so this forum seemed appropriate for just such things.

P.S. Johnson's new headphones are quite nice.

Sincerely,
Mark

Welcome to Afghanistan

"Are We There Yet ...No - Are We There Yet? ...No" H & B Simpson

Wow, I can no longer say greetings from Camp Shelby. Nope; now it's greetings from Southwest Asia. It was quite a voyage from Mississippi to Afghanistan. One of the guys on our team started a stopwatch as we left Mississippi; by the time we arrived in Afghanistan we clocked a total of just over forty three hours, with over eighteen hours in an airplane. I saw the sun rise and set at the oddest times during the trip, it was weird, and too many in-flight movies to count. The dreadful part of the whole jaunt was I, and a lot of guys on our team, had a hard time sleeping on the airplane. By the time we had reached our destination I logged in maybe a total of six hours of sleep, so not only were we exhausted, but the jet lag made for some interesting delusions. Here's the diamond in the rough though, look at the images below. The mountains we flew over were just stunning, that and we all arrived safely to our destination was a bonus as well.

After arriving at the airport we got in the back of some trucks, and prepared to move out to our first stop. Now it's okay for me to say that I am in Afghanistan, that's no huge secret, but I am not allowed to tell everyone what specific areas I am currently in. It keeps us safe, so please do not be offended by the ambiguity.

The movement from the airport to my first home was a pretty surreal journey, and sad at the same time. In addition to being physically exhausted, I am trying to make sense of the images my eyes are passing onto my brain. Not everyone here in Afghanistan was happy to see us, as we received cheers and jeers from the locals as we moved through the streets. All along the route, as you can see from the pictures, things are not quite as modern as we are used too. Poverty is something that the majority of the citizens of Afghanistan deal with on a daily basis, and now I got to see it first hand. It was heart wrenching to see children in among the trash and debris on the side of the roads looking for anything that may be valuable. It was like watching one those late night feed the children commercials, but now it was live. The houses I saw were primarily made out of earthen bricks, and most of them were in some state of disrepair. There were also shacks along the roadsides where merchants sold everything from tires to fruits, and anything in between. During my time at Camp Shelby I was shown images of this stuff on many occasions, but it certainly is not the same as seeing it with my own eyes. The people do need our help, and I am visually reminded why I am here. I hate the fact that I have to be away from my family, but I look forward with optimism that my being here may bring something positive to this country and its people.

One aspect of Afghanistan that was very obvious to all of us the second we stepped off the aircraft was that it's freaking hot here, I mean damn hot, I'm talking hot. The cool thing is, no pun intended, it's only going to get hotter. Sweet, but it's a dry heat, so no worries. Another interesting weather phenomenon we have observed here are dust storms. They just occur suddenly, the wind blows like crazy out of nowhere. As the wind blows it picks up a ton of dust and sand, making it hard to see anything around you. The locals call it the "120 days of winds", and some storms can be so severe that they will block the view of the mountains and sun. They are down right dangerous when they happen, forcing people to seek shelter much in the way we do during a tornado.

Well ... we'll be here at our first home for about a week. We have all the obligatory reception briefings from everyone here. Everyone telling us the same basic stuff we already knew one more time. Then we'll move on to the place where we will live for the next year. As soon as this occurs I will let you all know. For now; be cool and I will talk to you all again soon.

Regards,
Mark

Where there's water … There's life

"Have Gun … Will Travel" Unknown

Hi everyone. I am happy to report that I am finally ready to start work here in Afghanistan. After over a week of travel, to include many delays and layovers, I am in the place where the Army wants me to perform my craft. Ain't life sweet!!!

Let me tell you about the journey to get here, it's an awesome tale. The last time I left you I was at the starting point, as we had just landed in Afghanistan. We got stuck in stop number one for eight days, and let me tell you that got old real quick. There wasn't anything for us to do but wait, and so we spent our time sleeping, watching movies, or sitting up at the coffee shop watching television. Then one day we thought we were going to leave out of there, we sat at an airfield for all day waiting for a helicopter to arrive. When the bird did finally arrive, we were unable to get on the first flight; there were just not enough seats. We were told that the after the helicopter dropped off the first group, it would be back to pick us up, that never came to be. The next day a group of us was able to leave by convoy, and then the last four of us got a ride via helicopter.

The helicopter ride was remarkable; this country is absolutely stunning, as you can see from the pictures above and below. I have never seen countryside so diverse. There would be areas that were completely barren and right next to them areas that were completely fertile so full of life. Then I would look out the other side of the helicopter and see nothing but picturesque mountains. Most of the homes that people lived in were either made out of the earth, or carved right into it. It was amazing to see. I could also see many nomadic tribe people herding various livestock, mostly sheep, in search of those fertile areas. I was truly glad that I had the opportunity to see the country from this vantage point.

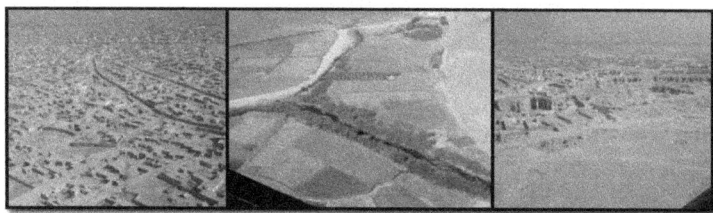

Once the helicopter dropped us off, and we got settle in to tour tent. I found out that this was not to be my last stop, and that I had yet another journey to go. This time, however, I was to travel by convoy and of course it was not one of the safest routes to travel. I was excited and nervous at the same time, especially after hearing the tales of my team members travels via convoy from the first stop. The next I loaded up my gear on the Humvee which I was to travel in, and got strapped into my seat. Fortunately I was lucky enough to get the front seat, but we were the last vehicle in the convoy. Once again the trip was from out of this world. There are very few developed roads in Afghanistan, and our trip did not find any of them. Pretty much the entire trek was on very dusty gravel roads. The dust was a very fine dust, and it reminded me of moon dust. In fact as we drove through the mountains, at times it seemed as if we were one the moon. It just got into everything, and at times it was difficult to breathe. It did make for some good boogers later though. The ride took us through the mountains, and most of the time when I looked out my window, all I could see was straight down. There was very little room for error on these roads. They were barely wide enough for two vehicles to pass, and so when we came upon a truck, one of us would have to move to the side to let the other pass. Most of the time we had the right of way, and I assume it was the menacing look of the Humvee with it's big guns that persuaded other driver to think this way.

After we made it though the precarious mountain pass I felt much better, and was able release the death grip I had on the door handle. Once tranquil, I really started to notice the countryside. The villages were filled with life. My favorite part of the journey was watching all the young children run to the side of the road, and give us the thumbs up as we drove by. I would make sure to return the salutation to as many of them as possible to acknowledge their efforts. I am instantly reminded of reason we are here. The children, as they are the innocent. In all the warfare that Afghanistan has seen over the last quarter of a century, they need the protection the most. The children that I see on this day are the generation that will hopefully actually get to live true freedom and independence when they are my age. That's what this whole mission is about, at least in my eyes.

Once we arrived at our new home, I was assigned barracks. Hey ... I got my own room. It is sweet, and I spent the afternoon building some furniture for it. Once I get all situated, I will most definitely post some pics of my new digs. For now I have to prepare for our first mission. I can't say a whole lot about it yet, but I get to meet some of our Afghan counter parts tomorrow, and I guess the meeting place is very striking. I look forward to filling you in when I can. Take care of each other.

Thank you Steve for the continued prayers, I think it's working so far. Also thanks to the Johnson's for the kind messages, you should email me pics of the family. I also want to make sure that I thank you Jack for the beautiful messages. I know I am a schmuck for not writing enough, but I will get on that in the very near future.

Best Wishes,
Mark

So Far ... So good

"And we've only just begun" K. Carpenter

Welcome back for this installment of the My Afghanistan Vacation Chronicles. So far things are going swimmingly here, and I am keeping quite busy. I've been doing quite a bit of traveling with our group, making sure that we meet with all the people that we are to interact with throughout the year. It has been quite exciting to get around the country a bit, and see this place that I will forever hold in my memory. It is a fascinating country. I got to meet with my Afghanistan counterparts, they are pictured above, and they were so excited to meet us. It is obvious that they really appreciate the help we are providing them, as far as training them to become a more modern army. It's no easy task though, and I am sure sometimes it will be frustrating. This is a proud army that has fought many wars, and they are certainly not afraid of a fight. One of the major obstacles that they face is that this army has never been truly united as one. There have been many warring factions here in Afghanistan, and now to try and pull it all together into one solid fighting force, it will certainly test their patience. No worries though, as they have made great strides in getting together so far, and I see nothing but continued success in the future. It's pretty awesome to be a part of this mission. As a new guy here, I have seen a lot of strange things, or at least what I thought was strange, so I have been asking a lot of questions. I want to take the time to express what I have learned thus far about the people of Afghanistan. One of the first things I noticed about the people is that they are meticulous stackers of stuff. The can stack anything such as rocks, firewood, and bags of freight on a truck, and it is so artfully done. Below is a firewood store and you can see that they definitely take time to

stack the wood, so it is all sorted out perfectly. Sorry it's a little blurry it was shot out of a moving vehicle. The people here also stack rocks to denote certain things. Some rocks may be stacked to show where a building foundation will go. Other rocks will be stacked to show tribal boundaries, so people here know where they can and can not go. The rocks below are stacked as markers for graves. When a Muslim passes away, the body must be buried within twenty four

hours of death, and the body must be pointed towards Mecca. Well; since the earth here is all rock and sand, the bodies are placed in shallow graves, and then the rocks are stacked on top of them. The people also may place a marker for remembrance, or a flag to denote what tribe they were from. I love the simplicity of their ceremony. The one thing that I did notice after passing several grave yards was that there were as many small graves as there were big ones. A reminder that child mortality here is higher than it should be. Two huge reasons exist for this, one is Afghanistan is a very rough and rugged country, and the other is a lack of medical technology.

Something else that is cool about the people of Afghanistan is that they are incredibly artful people. They love to decorate everything they own, and they do it with such vibrant colors. The people who drive trucks here are a prime example of what I am talking about. The picture below is of what we call a Jingle Truck.

It started out a normal truck, and then the drivers put all kinds of decorations on them. Some of the trucks are painted with beautiful murals or ornate ironwork, and others just have a lot of stuff hanging off them with colorful paint jobs. Each truck here is just as individualized as the driver operating it. It's interesting to see what the drivers do with these things. Why call them Jingle Trucks? Well; when all the stuff that's been added to truck gets moving down the road, it all bangs together making a jingle sound as the truck moves.

Along with the artistry part, the people of Afghanistan have some very skilled craftsmen. The people make the most beautiful woven goods, such as rugs and clothing. I have also seen some very impressive metal work and pottery, like the example below. The pictures are untouched, that is exactly what they look like. It was just really stunning work. They really seem to take pride in what they do. Some of may seem tacky to us, but that's the coolest thing about it, I seeing what is beautiful to them. Until next time, be cool.

Sincerely,
Mark

Working' for a Living

"I'm taking what they're giving because I'm working for a livin "
H. Lewis

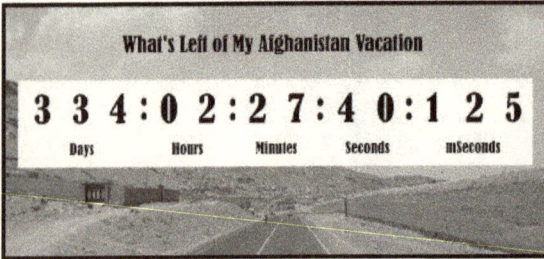

What's Left of My Afghanistan Vacation

3 3 4 : 0 2 : 2 7 : 4 0 : 1 2 5
Days   Hours   Minutes   Seconds   mSeconds

My job has definitely kept me busy around here so far, and I am constantly on the move trying to keep things running as best I can. My job mainly consists of keeping our computers and the network up and running, which is no easy task in the middle of nowhere. Of course the Army doesn't make things easy for me either. In classic military fashion, it is by far the most overly complex network in the world. Had I proposed this network topology in the civilian sector, I would have been chased out of town. I think the hardest part is the Army doesn't like to allow people at my level a lot of administrative access, so I have to rely a lot on our headquarters help desk, which is a day drive away, and dealing with those people has kept my receding hairline on the move. No matter what the obstacles, I have been able to keep things running fairly smooth … Matt and Dennis … you would be so proud. It's a long way from teaching Intro to Networking.

Another responsibility I have here is keeping all of our radio equipment up and running, and thankfully I have one

Sergeant in my charge who handles this aspect of my duties beautifully. He is indisputably the king of the radios around here, and he keeps our stuff running in spectacular fashion. We rely on the radios quite heavily since we have to travel a lot, and the radios are our lifeline to the world while we are in our convoys. I make sure to thank him quite a bit when I get the chance, and I even make sure I buy him lunch or dinner on occasion. For those of you who are asking the question in your heads right now, no we don't pay for meals, but it's the long standing joke for us here.

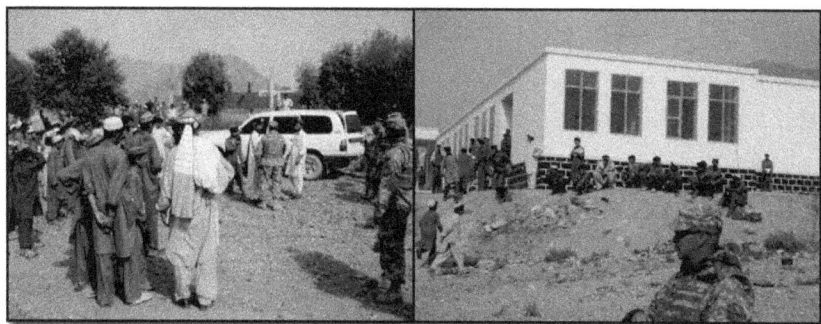

Now onto local Afghan News. The other day a group from our post went on a humanitarian mission. The mission was to stop at a school in a local village, and deliver supplies and gifts to the children. The school is a landmark school here in Afghanistan because the school not only teaches boys, which during Taliban rule boys were the only school attendants, but this school also teaches girls. To add; the school teaches both the boys and girls on the same campus. This is unheard of here, and is quite a progressive step for the people of the village. The boys and girls are separated while in school. The boys are taught in a beautiful new building, and the girls are taught in a tin shed out behind the school. Now I know this doesn't sound quite right, but it's a major step towards equality, and I am sure as time progresses this too will change. Because this is such a step away from Taliban rule, the school is obviously a target for the terrorists who wan to return to the days of old. The kids and their parents are quite brave for attending this school, so we like to help them out as much as possible by showing we have a presence there and bringing them supplies to help keep it going.

Another thing that we do as part of our humanitarian program is help the children who have been orphaned. The Army builds quite a bit of stuff around here in Afghanistan to help the people out such as wells, roads, schools, and yes orphanages.

There is one being completed in a village close to us, and it will be able to house three hundred children. The Army, with the help of other organizations, has been able to also provide the children with both winter and summer clothes. That's pretty awesome. On our post here there are Navy soldiers who collect school supplies, toys, and other kid type stuff and donate it to local schools and orphanages. We also have a Navy and Army contingency of medical professionals who go out into the community and provide medical clinics for the people of the surrounding villages. I think it would be great to help the Navy in getting this type of supplies to the children here. If anyone or group out there would like to help by sending anything, please leave a message here on the blog or email me, and I'll send you my address and more information. If I am going to be here a year, I want to do all I can to make it a good year for others too.

Let's talk about the wildlife, and I don't mean what we do on our off time. I finally ran into the alleged man killing camel spider. This ferocious beast, which I am sure you have all heard rumors about, is like nothing I have ever seen. It did indeed scare the shit out of me when I first saw it, but it certainly wasn't the twelve or eighteen inch super monster I had been hearing about. As you can see from the picture above, it is not the most pleasant creature to ever hang around with, but certainly no man killer. Boy was I relieved, as I had feared my first encounter with the deadly arachnid. I also did some research after my first encounter, and found out that the creature is not a true spider at all, it is a Solifugae, which is part of the arachnid family. It is not poisonous or has an anesthetic bite which allows them to eat their unsuspecting victim while they sleep. It doesn't eat the through the stomachs of camels, as they prefer smaller bugs and such. They are actually quite harmless to humans. I sleep much better at night knowing this, but I am not quite ready to start keeping them as pets on my nightstand. I thought you would all like to see what one looks like.

Well … that's all I have to report at the moment. Until next time is cool, I'd like to try and be cool myself, but as of late it has been over a hundred degrees during the day. Tough to stay cool. Talk to you all again soon.

Sincerely,
Mark

Home Sweet Hut

"I'm making notes for a book. It's to be a chronicle of our adventures on the island..." Professor Roy Hinkley

Hello all and it's good to chat with you again. I've been here for a just shy of fifty days now, and due to staying quite busy the time is ticking away relatively quickly.

In this post I thought I would show everyone where I work and live, as I am all sure you are curious about our accommodations. We live in buildings which are referred to as B-huts, and they are basically rectangle building constructed out of plywood. Thankfully all the buildings here are air conditioned, or this place could suck more than it already does. The B-hut I live in has been separated into four separate rooms, so I have a pretty good sized room to myself. It certainly isn't the Hilton, but it's not all bad. I do have my own room, which is mostly private; the walls do not go all the way up to the ceiling. The only downside to our accommodations is the wood used to construct them is from Pakistan, and they used some crazy chemicals to preserve the wood. I have been told they use everything from formaldehyde to kerosene. I am not sure what it is they use, but on occasion, especially during the heat of the day, the B-hut become quite noxious, almost to the point where you can't stay in them for long periods of time. I think sometimes that was the Army's plan all along, as the smell would preclude people from going to their huts for the much needed afternoon nap time. Another minor issue with the B-Huts is someone discovered that the ballasts in the fluorescent lights overheat and catch fire. Not a huge matter on its own, but when you live in formaldehyde soaked huts, I'm thinking … huge problem.

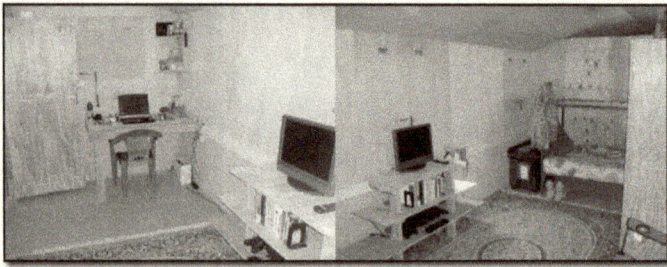

Now I don't want everyone at home thinking I'm living in some poison infested tinderbox, although it kind of is, but after time the smell goes away. It's just that our B-huts are brand new, and could use some airing out time. They are actually quite nice and relatively safe to live in. We even have smoke detectors and fire extinguishers within arms length if something does happen, so please don't worry. As you can see form the picture above, I have dressed mine up quite a bit, and made it as homey as possible.

The picture above is our office and this where all the business of the day takes place. The guy in the picture is SGT Schissel my workmate and friend, and he is by far the best non-signal signal guy I have ever had. Some days we spend a lot of time in the office fixing computers and radios, on other days we are out and about doing stuff on the road, and I think about missing my air conditioned office. Speaking of working out some cool computer problems, this one is for my computer geek friends and colleagues. The other day I came across several machines that had been ghosted with an obsolete image and no on knew what the password was. Well; so I tried to ghost them with a new image, and the image didn't have all the right drivers, so it failed miserably. Now I have quite the predicament on my hands, and I think to myself, what do I do now? I know I'll merely re-ghost them with the old image, and simply crack the password. Sounded simple to me at first inception, but truly no easy task, and then after a few of days of exhaustive research and practice I finally did it …. That's right friends; the war zone has made me a hacker. I'm not proud of it, but I can't wait to get home and demonstrate my new skills.

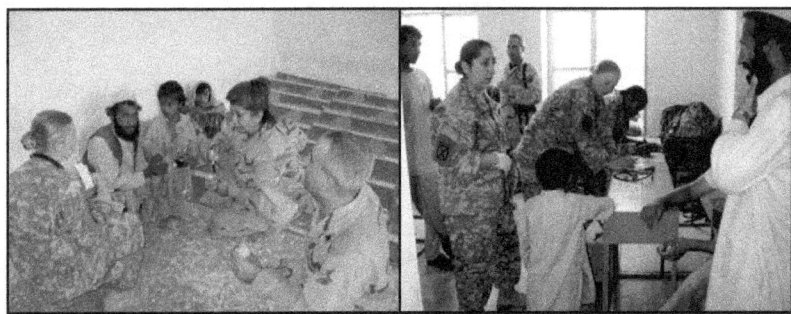

Some good news coming your way. The other day a bunch of soldiers from our camp, and other areas, went to a nearby village to do what's called a MEDCAP. It's were we get our hands on every medical professional in the area, and go to a nearby village to treat as many people as possible. I didn't get to go on this mission, but it's certainly something that I would like to do in the future. The soldiers that did go say that it's a great mission helping the people Afghanistan, but they say it's also an exhaustive day. Doesn't seem at times that we have enough people and time to treat all the people that show up. This MEDCAP there were over three hundred people treated, and the last one that was done treated over five hundred people. I think that's fantastic, and it part of winning the hearts and minds of the people of Afghanistan. I will certainly make sure I am on the next medical mission; it's one of the reasons I was excited about coming to here, as I knew the opportunity for humanitarian missions would present itself.

Now it's not all work and no play here in Afghanistan, as you can see from

the pictures below we try to have some fun too. Our old commander's

wife worked at a country club, and sent the camp here a bunch of golfing equipment. Clubs, tees, balls, and even hats with ball markers. The one major issue is of course; where in Afghanistan does one go golfing, especially since the one we are building isn't complete yet? Well … right on the protective barrier walls, of course, that's the perfect place to get some golf balls off into the atmosphere. And so that's what we did. We got all the golfing stuff, climbed up the barrier walls and spent some time in the afternoon launching golf balls into the desert. It was a brilliant time, although I noticed that my swing is a little rusty. Don't think of it as work.

I want to take a few lines to thank all of you that volunteered to send school supplies, as the children here need and will love to have anything you send. It's great that people want to help. I also want to take time to thank all of the people who have sent stuff to make life bearable. There are a couple of groups out there that have been sending us all kinds of goodies, and I want to let you know that the stuff is greatly appreciated.

Sincerely,
Mark

You Could Be One of These Guys

"Just Think...You Could Be One of These Guys"

Hello all, as always I hope that this posting reaches everyone who reads in good health and spirits. I was just sitting here; listening to the rain hit the roof of my office B-hut, thinking about how to express the last couple of weeks. I really like the sound the rain makes when it hits our huts, the metal roof creates a steel drum like music, pretty cool sound. It has rained here quite a bit in the last couple of weeks, sometimes so much that we have little ponds all around the compound. It's amazing how much it actually rains here; in what I thought was supposed to be a dry and waterless place. An amazing aspect of the rains here is how ingenious the Afghans are in harnessing the life giving quality of the water. I am not sure if I told you, but here in Afghanistan the people only cook with wood. They may use propane to heat water for tea, but everything else consumed must be cooked in a wood burning stove. I believe it is a custom derived from their Muslim teachings.

Well; in Afghanistan there are not a whole lot of trees around to just chop down and burn. However; when the rain washes down from the mountains it brings with it tons of trees and branches that once lived high on the mountains. As the water flows through the river beds, the children run all about the banks collecting the wood that has been deposited, and it is amazing how much has been dropped off by the water. As you have seen from a previous post, they collect and stack a lot of wood from this process, it's astonishing. I knew in the villages they had tons of wood all stacked up nice for sale, knowing that I hadn't seen many trees around, it was quite a mystery as to how all the wood got there. Until I saw the river process, I thought all the wood was imported from somewhere else, but after witnessing the collection method the shrouded mystery was unveiled. In the picture above a woman is collecting sticks now that the river has reduced into a stream.

Something else I also noticed when we drove through the villages was the large amount of produce for sale; they have everything from tomatoes to melons, and everything in between. Once again I wonder to myself how one grows such nice produce in a place that is supposed to be so desolate. The answer; the farmers of

Afghanistan are masters of irrigation. They use a process called flood irrigation. When it rains, it is usually huge amounts in a short amount of time. It usually floods the hell out of everything. What was once a dry river bed, in minutes will be a raging river out of nowhere. The farmers use earth, rocks, and whatever else they can get their hands on to divert the water into small fields they have prepared with little dirt walls around the perimeter, essentially creating a pool. The field have already been planted with whatever it was they wanted to grow, and they simply let the water sit there, keeping the plant life alive as it grows into the produce they sell at the markets. Using this process, and having plants that has been hybrid over years and years to tolerate the excessive amount of water all at once, they grow some pretty nice produce. Once again demonstrating a mastery of living in an environment some would consider hell on earth. Hopefully in the pictures you can see some of this process.

How did I learn all this you may ask yourself? Last week or so we drove half way across the country to visit some of our troops. For the most part the roads here are in horrible shape, and in other areas there are no roads at all, just a well defined paths. Years and years of neglect is reflected in the condition of these roads, in some places it is like driving on the moon, and surely demonstrates that this country needs its infrastructure rebuilt. Needless to say, riding hour upon hour in a Humvee, my body took quite a beating, and I was exhausted by the time we reached our destination. It's not all bad though, there is a huge highway project underway here, and construction crews are building new roads throughout the country. To include new roads, there are several new check points with beautiful new buildings, for the police to use to provide better security for those who travel.

We were fortunate enough to drive on some of the newly created highway. It was a beautiful stretch of road that wound itself though some stunning mountains; it almost reminded me of driving though the Rocky Mountains during the summer. So much so that I almost felt like we were on our way to some sort of National Guard Annual Training site, driving across the country like we did for so many summers. The day dream was rudely interrupted when the Afghan National Army soldiers traveling with us abruptly pulled over to the side of the road, and took off into the hills. I'm all of a sudden thinking we were taking fire from somewhere, I didn't recall hearing fire, and now I am wondering what the heck is going on. I see the other Americans traveling with us slowly emerge from their vehicles and casually stretch, so I am assured were not taking fire, but what's up with the ANA. Upon further investigation I figure out that this abrupt stop is actually a bathroom break, and all the ANA ran into the hills to take a leak. Were not in Kansas any more Toto and Afghanistan does not have roadside rest stops in which to just pull into to use the rest room and get a soda. So much for the daydream, I sure do miss home.

Anyhow, on this cross country journey I saw so much more Afghanistan than I had seen in the area we normally travel in. It was awesome to see these other aspects of the country that I had missed, and I certainly look forward to the next time I get to travel again. And other than our run in with the "rest stop", our travels were safe and event free. Driving around the country here is a lot like flying. When you land you like to kiss the ground thank God for allowing the plane to land safely. It is dangerous to travel here in Afghanistan; it's no secret that the enemy likes to target moving objects. However; in our armored Humvees, and an escort from the Afghan National Army, we are pretty assured to arrive at our destination event free, so please do not worry. To me, the risk is worth the travel; the experiences should not be missed or avoided.

Some other things I saw were a lot of sheep and goat herders moving their herds across the countryside. Some of the herders would move their animals right through the middle of the road, and there were a few of times I thought we were going to have to pay for a couple of brave but dumb sheep who thought it would be cool to try and challenge a Humvee to a game of chicken. I also saw my first herd of camels … finally after being here for over two months, camels; I was starting to wonder if they had them here at all. The rumor has been confirmed, they do exist here, and I have photographic proof. Another thing I saw; nomadic tribes moving across the countryside. Not sure where they were going, or where they came from, I guess that explains the whole nomadic thing. They would have their whole worlds packed on the back of a camel or mule, and occasionally I would see a little child riding in amongst their worldly possessions. That was a cute scene. I tell you though; none of the mules or camels I saw looked even mildly amused with the fact that they had to haul all that stuff. I think the most interesting thing about the nomads that I noticed was that the women did not wear the traditional burka that the rest of the women wear here. They would wear a head scarf, but no burka, virtually unseen by me here. However; when we passed them, they would look away and cover their faces. Curious.

Just to let those who so kindly donated supplies for the schools and orphanages know, we are planning a trip to visit an orphanage in the very near future to donate some of the stuff we have received. I will certainly make sure that I get plenty of pictures so everyone can see who is benefiting the most from our being here. I think that's our purest mission, which is helping to foster a safe and secure future for Afghanistan's children.

Also my apologies for this post being so long, if you are like me with a short attention span, this one may have tested your patience. It has just been busy enough here that I haven't had time to sit down and write until now, so I'm putting it down at once.

Until Next Time,
Mark

My Side of the Mountain

"We worry about what a child will become tomorrow, yet we forget that he is someone today".   Tauscher

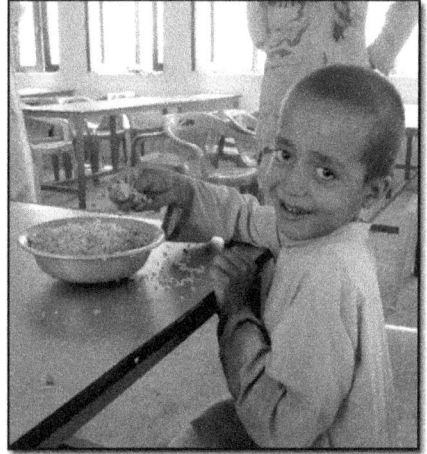

The other day we drove into town to drop our Corps of Engineers friends off at the airport; they were on their way to so much needed R and R. After we dropped off the engineers, we decided to stop into the hospital to see one of our soldiers. The soldier was having some pains in his abdomen, and the doctors were thinking he may have either an appendix issue or maybe kidney stones, but we wanted to make sure he was feeling alright. Once we got back into the ICU we saw our soldier, and he seemed to be resting quite peacefully. However; next to his bed, a little off to the side was another patient, a child. He had a ventilator responsible for his breathing, and various other assorted tubes leaving his body, all of which were obviously providing him life. He did not look well. The child appeared to be about twelve years old. I asked the surgeon what had happened to him, and I was told that the child had somehow come into contact with a landmine. The mine had robbed him of his hands, and shrapnel had ripped through his abdomen. When I asked the doctor how he was doing, he replied; "he has a long road of hope ahead of him." I assumed that meant that the outlook for this child is bleak. It was incredibly distressing to see such a young child lying there damn near lifeless. I think for what … so adults can have fundamental disagreements on religion, fight for political power, or fight for wealth. Whatever the hell the fight is over, it doesn't make sense sometimes. I am sure whatever the reasons, the child didn't care all that much. It forces me to hope that we make an impact here.

Enough of the melancholy; let me tell you about some of impact that we have made. A couple of days ago we were able to go on our humanitarian mission, finally after a couple of cancellations. It was a mix of emotions. It was fantastic to see the children, and bring a little something for them to smile about. It was also heartbreaking to see what conditions these children had to endure. The good certainly outweighed the bad in this case, and once again Afghanistan has amazed me. The facility was more than just an orphanage; it was a traditional school, with the addition of a care facility for those children without parents. During the day children from the local village attend the school, and in most respects it is treated like a normal Afghan school, with the exception of the classrooms. The classrooms are mixed sex; girls and boys are taught in the same classroom. Far more progressive than the last school we visited. The boys sit on one side of the room, while the girls sit on the other, but still in the same classroom with the same kind of desks. It was as if the children were kind of like equals, amazing.

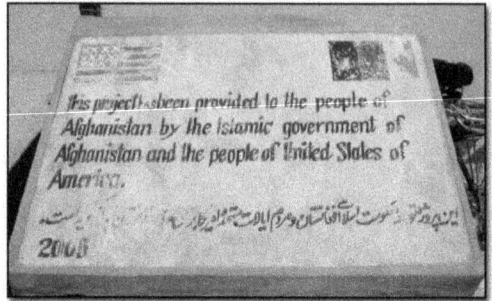

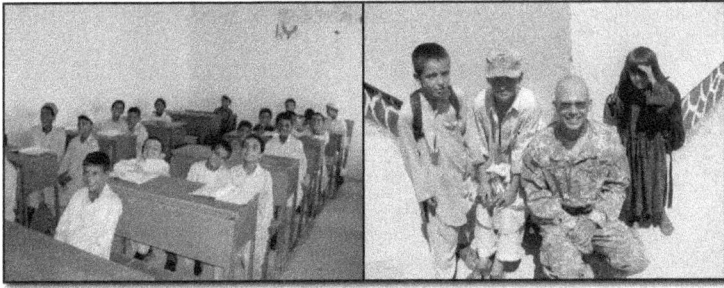

Then after the school day is done the village kids go home, and the children who have been orphaned live in another part of the building that has a dormitory for them. The school had a separate cafeteria building, which sits on top of a hill. The view from there was beautiful. We happened to stop by right about lunch time, and the children were dinning on a meal of flavored rice mixed with beans. I sat down at a table of boys and tried some, it wasn't too bad. That was it though; there was not enough money coming into the school to provide them much more to eat.

As we toured the school it was great to see that the children who have been orphaned get to intermingle with children who are not. At least the orphaned children are not all isolated together, all sharing the same sadness, they have an opportunity for some sort of normalcy. All of the kids were so excited to see us, and mostly because they knew we brought stuff. When I produced the large bag of fruit snacks, thank you for your donation Angie W, I was darn near mugged. They loved them. The Navy soldiers here took all the donations that we had received and created gift sacks for each child, which included much of the donated stuff that you all have sent me. They made the children line up, and they came up one or two at a time to receive their gift sacks. If we didn't do it this way it would have been mass chaos. It was priceless. I thank you, and the smiles of the children who received the stuff also proved that they appreciated it. We also brought some donated backpacks, clothes, and shoes for the children who may need some of that stuff. These donations were given to the school headmaster on the sly to be given out later to the children who may need them, simply to avoid embarrassing the children in front of their peers. Great idea.

One other thing we found out on our tour of the school was that the electrical generator provided was not operational, and the inhabitants had been living in darkness. We'll fix that. Overall the trip was brilliant, and I wish we could have stayed longer. We only stick around for an hour or so, we would hate to include the children if we became an impromptu target for the enemy. We will certainly go back in the future, and I also look forward to visiting other schools as we.

We always want to make sure that the schools in our area get equal treatment, as far as money and supplies are concerned. Thank you all for donating items for our visits, especially Angie H for organizing such a huge donation and continued support.

Since being in this country for as long as we have, we almost consider ourselves locals. One of the big local customs here is drinking the Chi. Chi is basically green tea, and the Afghans drink it throughout the day. It is a huge custom here, and it is considered quite rude to decline an invitation to drink chi when asked. Anytime we visit our Afghan National Army counterparts, I know that sometime during the visit we will stop talking shop, and sit down and enjoy some chi. They also usually offer some sort of snack along with the chi. We have snacked on everything from fresh raisins, almonds, Afghan candy, and other food stuffs that I did not recognize. All of it pretty good of course. Well; the other day we decided that the Comm. Section (Kyle and myself) needed to be a little more neighborly to the folks we work with. We asked a local Afghan national, Jaleel who works on our post, to go to town and get us all the fixin's to make chi. He brought us a propane stove, chi, glass teacups, and an aluminum teapot. All that was required to make chi, and as you can see in the picture below, we had our first ever morning chi party. Every morning, when it's possible, we make chi. We invite all of our neighbors to join, it's a good time to sit together and talk about stuff. I guess that's why it is such a popular custom here.

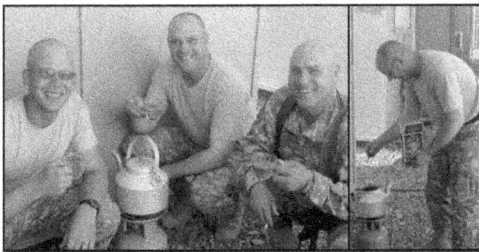

The last thing I wanted to tell you more about was the nomadic tribe's people we have seeing lately. I was curious when I first saw them, and I thought everyone else may be interested to know more about them. They are called the Koochi tribe, and they raise mostly goats, sheep, and sometimes camels. They live and herd their animals in the mountains during most part of the warm parts of the year. Then as it starts to get cold in the mountains they move their families and herds down out of the mountains to the warmer parts of the country. They used to have migration paths that they used, but because of the massive amount of landmines left by the Russians, they now mostly use the main road, which annoys the drivers, making them an unpopular people here. The Koochis are Muslim for the most part, but they also add in some folklore type teachings from their history. This adds to there unpopularity, as conservative Muslim religion doesn't really allow for additions to the tenants. Another reason they are not real well liked by the others in Afghanistan is that that they do not have traditional tribal boundaries. Boundaries are really important to most of the tribes here in Afghanistan, as this determines cast, wealth, and power, and they do not follow this traditional thinking. I think they are pretty cool, simply because they don't follow the social norms set by the populous. They are kind of like the hippies of Afghanistan. The pic below is a little fuzzy, I'll have to see if I can get better ones next time we go out, but that's how they live.

Once again thank you to everyone who has sent stuff for humanitarian missions, and the stuff you have sent to me. Each and every item is greatly appreciated, a little bit of home here makes the time a little easier to tolerate. If you would like a CD of pics from our mission, please remember to send me your mailing address in an email. Mom; those razors are perfect, just the kind I like. Matt; thanks for the OS X, I can't wait to experiment.

Sincerely,
Mark

Here's Your Computer Instructor: Pashto not Included

"You can't direct the wind, but you can adjust the sails" Anonymous

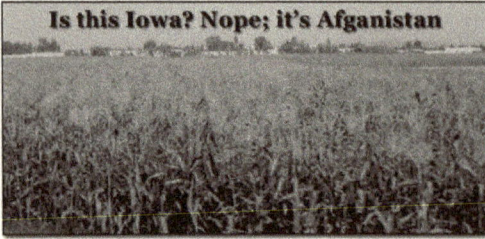

Is this Iowa? Nope; it's Afganistan

Welcome back everyone. I realize that it has been a while since the last posting, but it's been a crazy couple of weeks around here. One of those weeks we totally lost our Internet, for me not a good time, as it ran me pretty ragged. However; my network troubleshooting skills continue to improve, so that's good. I find it amazing how we have become so dependant on the Internet, even here in the middle of nowhere, in a country that considers an FM radio high tech. It wasn't too bad though, we joked around a lot about it, like everyone would constantly tell me the Internet was down and I was grounded to the FOB until it was fixed.

Now let me tell you what I have been doing lately. The Afghani National Army General that we work with had an imperative need for his soldiers become more computer literate. They were issued a

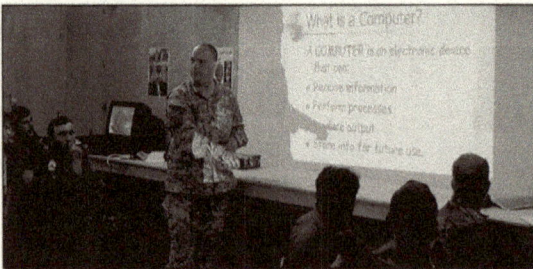

number of computers, and except for some mean games of pinball, the machines were simply collecting dust. Well; my bosses agreed with the General, who wouldn't, and took a look around the camp for an instructor. Hmmm … I wonder who can teach computer skills to our ANA brethren. The choice was pretty obvious. *Note to self; stop telling people what I do for a living on the civilian side.* With the help of my ever steadfast Comm. NCO SGT Schissel, we put together a hasty computer lab in our recreation room. Then I took some time to sit down and hammer out a curriculum, and usually this wouldn't have been a huge task for me, but now the rules have changed dramatically. This time the curriculum has to be customized for a group of students who have very little to no experience with a computer, but with this addition, the overall lack of mastery with the English language. The cherry on top of this academic sundae, the computers we are using also have nothing but English operating systems, English software, and English keyboards. You get the idea. The class is no longer a traditional introduction to computers 101, now it has become a hybrid introduction to computers 101 with how to speak English 101.

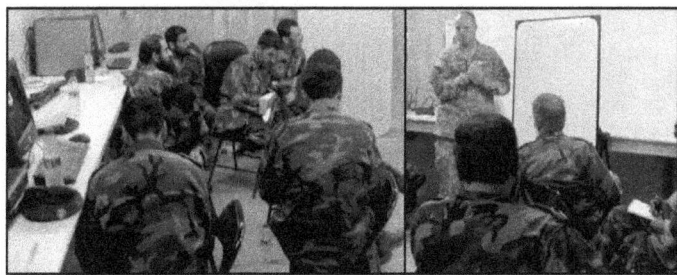

The classes have been challenging for both the ANA and myself, but I think more so for the interpreters. I have been giving them the curriculum in advance, so they have time to go through and find translations to words that the Pashto language doesn't normally have. There is so much computer jargon that we have to use in the classes and for the interpreters finding words that closely match the jargon has proven to be pretty difficult. After a couple of nervous first sessions for all parties involved, the classes have been going off without much of a hitch. They have been a lot of fun for us to be a part of, and it's been pretty awesome to see the ANA trying something so new and foreign. They have really taken to the machines quite well, and I think given more time and practice, they will be more than able to use their computers to increase their efficiency. Another brilliant byproduct of teaching the classes is that I have been in contact with so many more of the Afghan soldiers than before, and I get to continue to sharpen my skills as an instructor. It's a win / win situation for all. The ANA are always so gracious and appreciative after the class, makes me miss work a bit.

It's time to give everyone out there a tour of our local shopping center. I thought since I always talk about going to the mart to buy various local items that I would show you exactly what I am talking about. I am also very excited to show everyone the newest addition to our shopping experience, and that is our very own Afghan bakery. The bakery makes the traditional unleavened bread called Noni, so far it is the only product they make, but it does comes in three flavors.

Cinnamon is my favorite, but they also make garlic flavored, and a plain version of the bread. Every once in a while when we feel like making morning Chi, we'll go down to the bakery and get some of the bread; it is the perfect addition for morning tea. As far of the rest of the shops are concerned, you can see that we can get a variety of products. The shops usually carry anything that we would need, but if we had a particular need they couldn't meet immediately, the shop owners would bring us whatever we need the very next day if possible. They are quite accommodating. Usually the shops at bigger camps here in Afghanistan have a focus, such as having all types of tech items. At those you can get anything from a fan to cool your CPU to a mouse pad from a company you've never heard of. Most of the tech items are cheap Chinese knock-off of more expensive Chinese products we would normally buy in the US. Example: we may buy a mouse with the IBM logo back home from the local Best Buy, at the Afghan mart you may buy an exact looking version of the same mouse, but the logo may say IBN. Whenever you buy something, the statement "buyers beware" is definitely true, but they are pretty good at exchanging items that don't work.

Some of the shops may focus on movies and television DVD's, and they'll have anything you can possibly think of wanting to watch. You have to be careful though; copyright laws here don't exist, so you never know if you are getting a good copy of your movie. I have bought movies that you can hear people coughing, or the camera guy can't hold his Handy-Cam too steady, and my all time favorite you'll see someone get up to go get some popcorn. For two to three bucks a piece, what the hell. Then there are the shops that focus on selling local Afghan products such as carpets and local arts and crafts. Because we are a small camp our particular shops seem to carry a variety of everything, quite an eclectic collection of stuff is offered. Its fun to shop because you get to play the haggling game and meeting the locals who run the shops is always interesting. We like having our own shopping center, it almost like being at home and cruising down to the local mini-mall, and we don't have to convoy to get there.

Since I have shown everyone my living quarters, I thought I would also show you around a typical Afghan home. The typical Afghan home that we see in our area of the country is usually surrounded by massive walls made out of stone, earth, and sometimes brick. The structures are very fort like in appearance as you can see in the pictures. It is pretty obvious that many years of invasions and war has influenced the design of an Afghan home considerably. The immense walls also serve another purpose; it is one of very few places where a traditional Muslim woman does not have to wear her Burhka. Since no "foreign" men can see her over the high walls, she is not required to hide herself. The courtyard area within walls is called a haweley, and with all the available space you may see a garden of fruits and vegetables. There are usually a couple of buildings within the haweley; one would be the living quarters, or koh, depending on how many generations that live within the same compound there may be a couple of these. The kitchen, or pakhlandzay, is a separate building because they cook with wood. Don't want to turn the koh into a smokehouse.

For larger compounds one may also see a small Mosque, and some have their own private well. It's interesting to watch them build the high walls, what they do is dig a hole in the ground and fill it with water. Then a man will fill a shovel full of the mud mixture and flip it up to a guy on a scaffold. He then will hand pack the mud in about two foot layers, and after a few layers, you have a wall. In our area there is a lot of construction, which is great, as it is demonstrates prosperity and rebuilding. We also see a lot of construction in the cities, but they use more modern materials and construction techniques to build there.

Well; I hope you enjoyed the tour. Next time we get together I'll make sure to tell you all about Ramadan, it is a huge holy time of year for Muslims, and it's right around the corner. I'm eager to learn all about it. Be good to each other, and I will chat with you all soon. I also once again want to make sure I thank everyone for the almost overwhelming response to my request for school supplies. To date we have collected over forty boxes of supplies, and I am expecting quite a few more. I am looking forward to seeing how many boxes we collect at the end of this year. I think it will be quite a contribution, and I really want to make sure that I thank all of the people who read the Blog and responded. It's pretty awesome, and all the people who have received our donations are truly appreciative.

Sincerely,
Mark

The Book of the Done Cow, and Other Assorted Tails

"Cows have no Business in Horse Play"   Jamaican Proverb

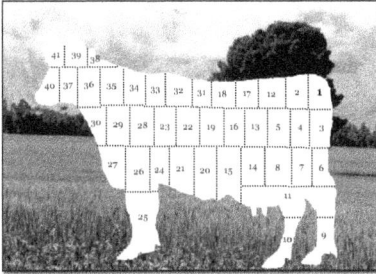

Hey … Welcome back everyone. We just clicked over four months of completed time in country. Sweet. We are over a third of the way done, and only thirty four more Steak Days to go until we are home. What is a Steak Day you ask? Well; instead of counting just days, which by the way is somewhere around two hundred thirty eight days, seventeen hours, fourteen minutes, and fifty seven seconds, but who's counting, we try to count down other events to make things a bit more interesting. Every Friday we have Steak and Lobster night, and every time Friday rolled around we would make a big deal about it being steak night. It's the perfect day to count because it kind of marks the end of each week, so I got all crazy into the Photoshop one day, and took a cow and divided it up into 41 pieces. When I got the crazy idea that's all the steak days that were left, and then each week I add another piece back onto the cow. We have a staff meeting everyday, and one Friday I got the crazy notion that it would be funny to unveil the cow slide I created as part of my brief. It's the picture you saw above. When my bosses first saw it, I wasn't quite sure what they thought of it, but there were enough giggles from the rest of the staff, that the slide has become a semi-regular part of my Friday brief. We're always trying to figure out what kind of stuff we cant get away with around here to break up the monotony just a bit, and I am sure you all know who leads the charge on this challenge.

It's been business as usual for us here, and we have continued to teach away for the ANA. Let me tell you; business has been good for us. When we first started, we were just teaching the Brigade staff how to use their computers. Somehow word got out that they may actually be able to use these machines for things other than holding their doors open once they have complete the course, and so other groups wanted to get in on the action. We have now included two additional ANA groups to our roster, which is great because it keeps us busy, and it helps them automate their world. I always say we because it takes a group effort to deliver the curriculum. I always have a minimum of three interpreters for about a ten to twelve person class, and SGT Schissel is always right at my side, available to help in any way possible. I should say that he is quite the instructor himself, as he has conducted many a radio class for the US Brigade staff, and just the other day he conducted radio classes for the ANA security force we have here on camp. Needless to say it has been challenging to create a curriculum that meets the specific needs of this particular group of students, but it has also strengthened and reenergized the way I look at instructing. The experience has been pretty cool thus far, which brings me to sad

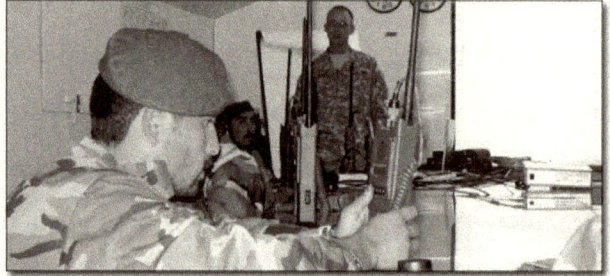

part of this posting. I am slated to be relocated elsewhere in country soon. Yup; moving to another place, and so I have to leave this entire splendor behind. To tell you the truth, I am not happy about the move at all. We have carved quite a niche into this little chuck of Afghanistan we call home, and I am going to hate to leave it behind. When we first stepped foot into the Commo shop it was an utter disaster, but we have put a lot of effort into getting the place running pretty darn smoothly, so it will be pretty tough to hand it off to the next guy. Thankfully; I know who my replacement is, we trained at Camp Shelby together, and I know he will certainly continue the trend. Another reason why I am going dislike leaving is SGT Schissel is remaining here. We have pretty much been inseparable since we started working together, and I absolutely appreciate his work ethic and admire his sense of humor. For not being a school trained commo guy, he would certainly makes the real commo guys quite proud with his mad skills. It's not all bad though, the good news is that the move I am making is an upward move, and I will be the new Corps Signal Officer. That's cool.

Well enough of the sad, let's see what else has been going on around here. The last couple of weeks have been pretty quiet around here, which is a good thing.

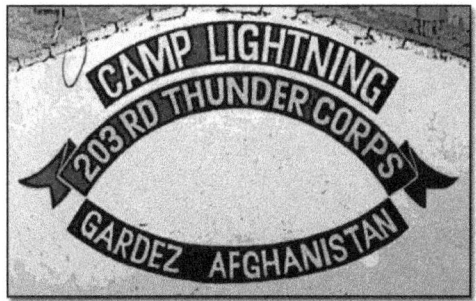

For Muslims it is a very holy time of year called Ramadan. Ramadan starts on the ninth lunar month of the Muslim calendar, and goes for one complete lunar cycle, about twenty eight days. It is the celebration of the Prophet Muhammad receiving the holy Qu'ran from Allah (God). During the entire month the Muslims dedicate themselves fully into their faith, and leave behind some of their everyday concerns. During this month the ANA do not like to work throughout the day, and most times quit work in the early after, if they go to work at all, which will explain some of the peacefulness around here. During the days of Ramadan, starting from sun up and finishing at sundown, the Muslims do not eat. As part of the fast they also refrain from drinking anything, smoking, and sex. The idea is the person can take this time to contemplate his relationship with Allah, and the lack of food and drink is to concentrate on their thoughts. During each day they will pray up to five times a day, some of the prayer time lasting over an hour, again part of that reflection.

At the end of the day, as the sun is setting, they perform a long special evening prayer called the Taraweeh, and then they will then eat a large meal called the Iftar. To conclude the evenings a lot of Muslims may spend the time meeting with family and friends, to tighten those family bonds and strengthen relationships. Then they start the practice all over again as the next morning approaches. Other things that a Muslim must observe during this time, more than usual, are the way they act towards each other. They can not treat other Muslims badly, talk or gossip about others, lie, or be greedy. If they do any of these things, then the time they have spent during the day fasting and praying was basically wasted, and they cannot receive any of the good that should come from it. Muslims also believe that on the last night of the month of Ramadan, about the twenty seventh day, marks the actual time that Muhammad received the word form Allah, and in modern day this is when Allah will determine what the world will be like for the next year. That is why is it so important to be reverent to holiday, as it dictates what the next whole year will be like. To finish off the month long observance, Muslims will rejoice in huge fashion with a three day celebration called Eid, where they will eat huge meals, celebrate with family and friends, and some villages even have fairs.

When Ramadan started, I basically knew nothing of the holiday, and so I went right over to my favorite interpreters to get the scoop on what it was all about. They are always so helpful in trying to give me insight into the new things we experience here. We were told that Ramadan should be a very peaceful time in Afghanistan because it is important that Muslims treat other Muslims with well. Sadly, even the most peaceful of celebrations the bad guys seem to ruin. We thought that maybe they would try and attack us more to make a statement, and leave their own brethren alone, but sadly that hasn't happen. The bad dudes are still out there hurting people who support stability and progress in Afghanistan, and of course they are sloppy at it, so there have civilians hurt in the process too. It simply goes to show that the bad guys do not hold their Muslim religion in very high esteem as they claim to. Once again they have proven that it is

not a holy war, but it is more of a political war. A time when Muslims are supposed to respect and love each other, these guys are out there carrying on business as usual. To me it is incredibly sad to see this happen. However; of course it is time for the upswing, the good news moment. When the bad guys do such things during this very holy time, they tend to lose favor within the communities that may have supported them in the past. Here's something interesting about this country. There are basically two leaders in each village; the elected official is one, and the religious leader (Mullah) is the other. When the Governor of a village speaks, the people may or may not listen to depending on how they feel about the particular topic. However; when a Mullah speaks, most people listen. His wisdom and religious knowledge are held in very high esteem by the people, and he is a well respected man. Well; when the bad guys decide that during a religious holiday it's a good time to bad things, this angers the Mullah, and he may denounce the bad group to the villagers. The people will almost

always follow suit, and the bad guys no longer have safe haven in that village. This is good news for us, and the people of Afghanistan, who want to rid their country of this evil. The real challenge a lot of the time, because the bad guys use religion as a guise for their war, it is tough to express to the Mullahs that these are bad people. Thankfully they help us on occasion. Anyhoo,; as the end of Ramadan draws near, I grow increasingly excited to see what the three day celebration will be like, and I will certainly tell you all about the next time we meet. By the way; above is a picture of a few of my favorite interpreters.

Another new development here at our slice of heaven, is we now have Internet in our huts. It is fantastic, and those that I have chatted with will attest to this fact, to have this available to us. It is a sweet satellite system from a company out of India, and the cost is pretty reasonable. I have spent the last three weekend's video chatting with my family as long as I can. It is great to actually see them, and more importantly, they can see me. My boys so love computer time with dad, I know this will help bridge some of that gap that is between us. The speed is not mega fast by any means, but I have a dedicated line reaching blazing speeds of 128kbs. Plenty enough speed to video conference, and play some online checkers with my six year old. If you see me online, that is me, and don't hesitate to stop in and say hello. I appreciate the conversations very much; it is nice to catch up on what is going on at the home front. The only real problem with the chatting thing is that we are nine and a half hours ahead of you guys, so synching up out times without either party losing too much sleep can be a bit of a challenge. To tell you the truth, I stay up late sometimes to talk home, and I may show up a couple of minutes late for work. I don't think my boss minds too much, that simply because he hasn't caught me yet. Don't tell anyone.

Well; that's about it for now, nothing else significant to report here. Just want to make sure everyone knows that we are doing fine. Everyone is healthy, wealthy, and wise, so nothing to worry about here. I also want to make sure that I give everyone the thumbs up for all the nice things that have been sent, care packages and school supplies, they are truly appreciated. It's funny; even when I know the box is full of school supplies, I still get excited about receiving something from home. Thanks everyone for participating. Mom Sankot; thanks for the nice words on the Blog, it's good to hear that it is enjoyed by all. Johnsons; as usual you have me in your prayers, and it must be working, so keep up the good work. I appreciate the emails. Renae; keep the boat afloat, I'll be home before you know it. I may just let you keep the helm though. Talk to everyone soon, and be good to each other.

Sincerely,
Mark

Movin' on Up . . . To a de-lux apartment in the sky.

"Not houses finely roofed, or the stones of walls well built, make the city, but men able to use their opportunity."   *Alcaeus*

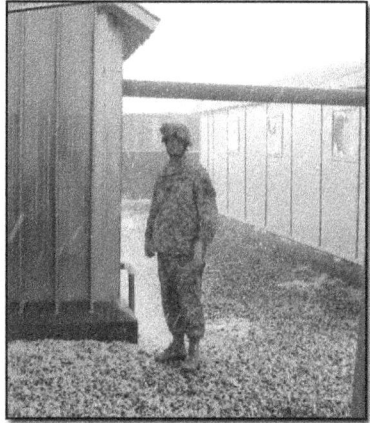

Welcome back all and I hope this post reaches everyone in good health and spirits. We have just completed five whole months, and it seems like the time has been flying by recently. Right around the corner is the Holiday season, and I am excited as we near this time of year. Not so much for the holidays themselves, as I am sure they will be a bit depressing, being away from home and all. They will, however, signify that half of this journey has been completed, and from that point on we are on the downhill slide. I'm always looking forward to the next milestone, counting down steak days as it were. To remind us of the impending holiday season, Mother Nature decided to give us a little show. About a week or so ago we had this hailacious hail storm, and as you can see from the pictures above and below, a lot of hail fell from the sky. I figured

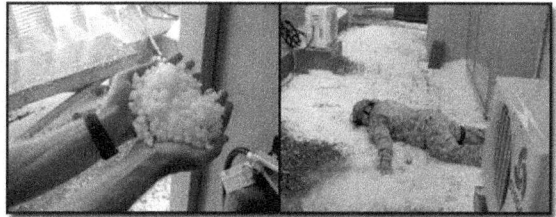

this is a good time to remind myself of how fragile the human body is, so I stood out in the hail to see if I could handle a beating from Mother Natured for one minute. Well; I am sad to report that I didn't make it; you'd be amazed how much that hail hurt. I know its nuts; but what the hail else am I going to do for fun around here? I haven't made my big move yet, but it is still planned for sometime in the future. Before I can move; I've got some business to finish here, and I'll tell you all about it.

Things here have resumed its usual nutty pace, and we are busier than ever now that Ramadan and the Eid celebration have concluded. The ANA are slowly but surely returning from visiting their family and friends, and it's back to work for us all. For about a year now the Corps of Engineers have been overseeing the construction of a brand new ANA camp right in our back yard. The camp is absolutely beautiful, and everything is shiny brand new. The ANA are very excited about the camp because they have been spread out all over the place, and their conditions have not been all that glamorous. The new camp is modeled after other new camps that have been built here in Afghanistan, but has also included a lot of improvements that were learned from the other camps as they have been inhabited. What's really cool about their new place is it is totally self sustaining. It can produce its own electricity, so no one is sitting in the dark. It also has a water purification plant, and a sewage treatment plant. The new camp does a couple of good things for the ANA, first off, it gives them a brand new home with a consolidated headquarters, making management of the troops a much easier task. It also brings with it legitimacy that the Army of Afghanistan is the governments' officially recognized force. The construction and maintenance of the facilities have also help to provide a lot of locals with steady work, and that should be a trend that will continue as the camp is lived in. It is also an advantage to us because we no longer have to drive all over the place to go visit with our ANA counterparts, now they are right next door. This is going to give us a lot more face time with them, and allow us to do a lot more mentoring.

Moving day has been a long time coming, and we have been planning it for sometime now, but we are glad it is finally here. It reminds of the time of year when all the college kids are moving into the dorms. There are pick-up

trucks everywhere, with stacks of home goods in the back, parked all over the place. I see nothing but the excited and anxious faces of the new residents eagerly unloading their worldly possessions into their new homes. It is an awesome time. SGT Schissel and I have been helping the Communications section set up their antennas and communications center, so they can be in touch with the rest of the units in the country. The move hasn't been totally flawless thus far, and as our ANA counterparts have learned that not all soldiers receive an office. To the higher ranking soldiers an office is a sign of status, and they take great pride in having an office space to call their own. Not having an office to them means they are not as important. There have been quarrels within the communications section over the one office that has been designated as theirs. Within the section they have a huge office space in which they have to share, but only one actual office. Unacceptable. I have spent some of my mentoring time as a mediator, trying to figure out how we are going to solve this problem. We've come up with some interesting solutions, but the one that makes the most sense and should solve the problem, is we are going to be adding a new wall to the new building to create another office. This should make the two majors involved in the dispute happy. I hope. We have also had disruptions in water and electricity, neither service being on at times, making for some smelly conditions. All these matters will certainly work themselves out in time, although with the office situation, there may be some hurt feeling in the end. Other than the expected growing pains everything has been going pretty well, and I am sure as time passes on the camp will grow and be an important fixture within the surrounding communities.

There are some other downsides to the ANA receiving their new camp, and that is with all the new Afghan soldiers that are moving our way, with them will be their mentors in tow. The number of soldiers on the American side is also expected to grow, and well, there are just not enough huts to go around. Over the past couple of weeks we have had a construction crew, led by the awesome Iowan Maj. Winekauf, and they have been heading up a project to make more room in our existing huts. What this mean for me? Well; the walls of Castle Bromwich will come crumbling down, and they will be replaced by a much smaller and efficient Condo Bromwich. Also; for a time all of our facilities, such as the chow hall and bathrooms, will be much more cramped. Thankfully our facilities folks are all over it, and are already starting construction on larger amenities to accommodate all of the new townspeople expected to arrive. The short term will be a little uncomfortable, but long term, the American side of our slice of heaven too will be a really nice place to live while on vacation here in Afghanistan. It's kind of sad that I will not be able to be around long enough to see this whole thing come together. It is like someone has taken the last chapter of a book I was reading, and now I will not know how it ends. Kind of sucks, but that is the way of the Army; no one stays in one place too long. I do look forward to the challenges of the future, and what my new position may hold for me, but frankly I don't care what I do or where I go. I just want to finish out my vacation, and get home to the safety of my classrooms. I so long for that day.

Our humanitarian supplies collection efforts have been going well, and I have no one to thank but all of you that sent boxes of supplies. SGT Schissel and I have collected over sixty-five boxes, and now that our major operations in this area have slowed a bit, we plan to get back into the distribution of supplies to the locals. We are also hoping to run some medical clinics within the new ANA camp, and that's always an opportunity to give out supplies to the locals when they come to visit the doctors. SGT Schissel will continue to distribute boxes that we receive after I leave this area. I plan to get involved with any efforts they may have at my new home and if none exists, which I am pretty sure they do, but if not I will just go ahead and start one. I do appreciate everything that all of the folks back home have sent over the time I have been here so far. Thank you all. Also; thanks Matt for the quick PHP lesson, it helped a lot, and I am sure I will ask for more help in the future. A hearty hello to everyone at the college, and at the Guard, I appreciate all the emails and letters. Everyone be good to each other, and I will talk to you all again soon.

Sincerely,
Mark

The Beginning of the Second Half; New Game....

"The world is round and the place which may seem like the end may also be only the beginning."   *Ivy Baker Priest*

A hearty and happy Thanksgiving day to everyone. I hope that everyone is having a pleasant holiday season with family and friends, and simply enjoying the time to get together. We had our big T-day celebration here, the Colonel bought some real turkeys, instead of the usual processed stuff we get, and deep fat fried them for the troops. It was a good meal, and I actually took some time to sit down and watch some football, something I haven't really done yet this year. Hope the Bengals are doing well, last I checked they were doing pretty good. Although I have yet to see them play this season, I hope to catch a game of theirs soon. As time markers go; Thanksgiving is a good one to place on the milestone list because it is the Holiday that marks one hundred and ninety-nine days to go. Sweet; as we are finally under the two hundred day mark. Alrighty then; let's get on to the updating.

Well; I have made the move to my new home now. It was cool because some of my Iowa buddies were the ones that made the convoy down to come get me. It was good to see those guys, as it has been some time since I have seen some of the members of the Iowa team. My new home is a staggering four thousand more feet up into the mountains than I was before. At Khowst the elevation is about four thousand feet, and now at my new residence, we are an incredible eight thousand feet in the air. This makes the air much thinner, and I find myself trying to catch my breath all the time. The guys here say it takes a couple of months to get used to the high altitude, and that I shouldn't try and rush my acclimation. I take that as I should not have to worry about doing PT for a while, as I don't want to rush things, but I get the feeling my new boss won't see things the same way. The moderate temperatures that I have grown accustomed to will no longer exist here, in fact it is just plain cold, and the other night we had snow falling from the sky. I know I shouldn't complain, I am from Iowa after all and I should be used to this, but I didn't expect the weather to be like this on my vacation. Of course there is always the plus side; the scenery here is stunning, as you can see from the pictures. We are surrounded by huge mountains, and there is already snow capping of the tops. It is absolutely picturesque, and every morning I have been here so far I take a few minutes to just stare at the mountains, make sure I engrain the scenery into my memory. I doubt there are many places like this on earth. Although my new home is pretty cool, no pun intended, I sure am going to miss Khowst. We did a lot of good work there, and I made a lot of fine friends, especially my commo NCO SGT Schissel.

The last thing I am going to miss about my last residence is being able to go the shops. I was pretty able to get

anything I wanted from those guys. I would just tell them what I need, and they would usually have it for me in a day or to. That was very convenient. My new habitat doesn't have a row of stores out front, so getting things I may need is going to be a little trickier. Of course there is always a good side to everything. On the ANA side of my new home there is a little shop. It doesn't have all the cool stuff of my old shops, but what it does have is a little tiny restaurant inside, and there they make these fresh French fries. They are an awesome treat, and really hit the spot about mid morning. The come out a really golden brown color, and when I say golden, I mean an oddly golden color. Must mean they are deep fried in some sort of interesting oil, probably used motor oil. It's just better not to ask what they use, and enjoy the snack. The other morning we had some fries right out of the oil, and we washed it down with a Chinese imitation of Red Bull. Yummy. As the old beer commercial used to go … "It just doesn't get any better than this."

The few days I have been here have been great thus far, and I have met my new Afghan National Army counterpart. He is a very pleasant, calm, and focused fellow who seems genuinely interested in the success of his signal section. Unlike my last counterpart, who also was focused on the success of his signal section, but he went about business in the exact opposite manner. He was a very animated, humorous, and sometimes just a crazy guy, and I never knew what to expect from him on a day to day basis. I am really going to miss him though, probably because he was more like me; we both have a kind of unorthodox management style. We got along pretty well, and I wish him nothing but continued success as he progresses towards the future. I will also enjoy my new counterpart, and I think he will be a nice and welcomed change that I look forward too. I have also spent some time meeting all my new counterparts' staff, and just like my guys in Khowst, they are sad to hear that their mentor is leaving them. It's nice to know that they liked the last mentor, but also presents me with challenge of filling his shoes, and making sure that I give them the same tools for success as my predecessor did. The signal staffs, and for the most part all the ANA soldiers I have met thus far, are all pretty hard working guys who really believe in what they are doing. They all want to see a safe and free Afghanistan, but I think it is going to take

time. As always; I hope that I am part of bringing that change about.

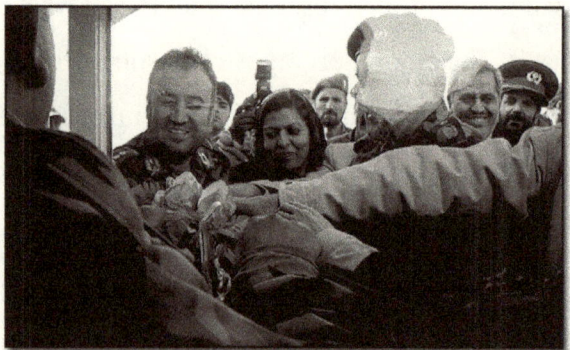

On the second day here since my arrival there was a brand new hospital opening. The new hospital can hold up to one hundred patients, and is chocked full of state of the art diagnosis equipment. The hospital has regular care, a trauma center, and even includes dental and eye clinics, pretty much unheard of here in Afghanistan. It is an impressive facility to care for soldiers, police, their families, and also local Afghans from the surrounding communities. This hospital is only the second of its kind here in Afghanistan, but it is a step in the right direction to providing health care for all the peoples of Afghanistan. The hospital opening drew all kinds of attention too; there were all kinds of political and religious dignitaries from the Capital city of Kabul and the local cities here. It was really cool to see all these people out in support of the hospital.

During the opening ceremony there was the traditional ribbon cutting, a ton of speeches from the VIPs, and the always popular cow slaughtering. I wasn't quite ready to witness the slaughtering of a cow,

so I decided to hide in the VIP room while this occurred. Of course after the ceremony I had to check out the pictures, just to

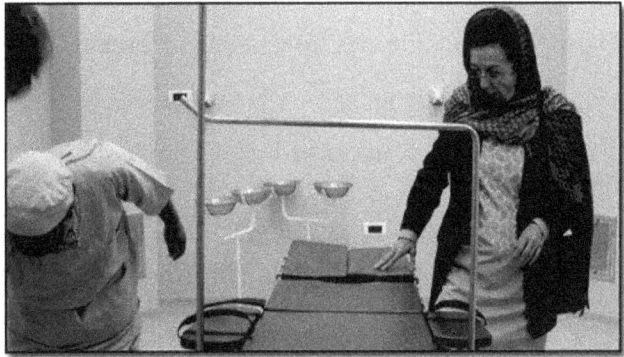

get an idea of how the ceremony was carried out. The idea behind the slaughtering of the cow was not really to make the hospital and its ground sacred, which is what I thought at first. The idea is that the sacrificed blood of the cow is drained into the earth and covered, taking it with it all the bad things that could occur at the hospital. With the bad things buried nothing but good will happen above ground where the building of the hospital is. At least this is what I gathered from my new interpreter, so hopefully I understood him okay. He is a pretty cool guy, but as with all the interpreters I have worked with, it takes time to fully understand how they interpret. It was either that, or he was trying to tell me that this is their idea of the steak night … could go either way on that one. They did however fully butcher the cow right there on the spot, and I am pretty sure was eaten soon after that. I was going to post a pic or two of the ceremony for you guys, but I though I'd better not, I remembered that there are kids out there reading this too. After the whole ceremony we had lunch with all the attendees, and the first thing I asked was what we were eating, much to my relief we were not eating the freshly sacrificed animal. Somehow that made it easier to enjoy the lunch, and it was quite the spread, a lot of new foods that I have never tried before and a couple a will never try again. My experiences with Afghan cuisine have always been pretty good so far, but they all can't be winners, there were a couple of the dishes that I do not wish to try again. All in all; it was a pretty sweet day, especially for the people of Afghanistan.

For my next adventure I am off to the Capital city of Kabul, where I will be attending a conference for all of the signal officers here in

Afghanistan. It is actually for the ANA, but we are going to tag along to see what going on in Afghan Army communications, as it will help us help them move in the right direction. It should prove to be an interesting time. I am excited about going to the big city; I haven't been there since we arrived in country. When I get back here; I'll make sure to tell you all about it. Once again I hope you all are having a nice Thanksgiving, and I'll talk to you all soon.

Sincerely,
Mark

The Ghost of General Lee Right Here in Afghanistan

"Did you know that there's a man living in our closet?" "So?" "Well why is he in there?" "Well why are you in there? ..." Real Genius

Hi everyone. I trust that the Holiday season is treating you all well thus far. It's beginning to look a lot like Christmas around here. We have had a lot of snow as of late, as you can see in the

pictures, and people are decorating their various areas with all sorts of Christmas paraphernalia. Of course it won't be the same as being home, but we will make the most of the season. The nice thing is that we have an extended "family" here, and we're all going through the same thing, so we all have each other to lean on when times may get sad. I have already received quite a few gifts from home, but I promised not to open them until Christmas, not an easy task for me. I was never good at waiting, but I will do my best to save the surprise. The good news is we passed the official halfway point the other day, and now we begin the count down to homecoming. It's nice to know that half of my vacation is complete; mentally it doesn't seem as insurmountable as it once did. The transition to my new home has been going well, and I have been fortunate enough to have a lot of help from my predecessor on how this job is done. The job will be all right, and I think it will be entertaining working at the Corps level. I sense I also have a lot of learning to do, as this job has a lot more moving pieces to it. Anyhoo, let me tell you what's been going on sine the last time we chatted.

Last week I was able to go to the Ministry of Defense (MOD), Headquarters for the Afghan National Army (ANA), for a conference of all the Afghan Signal Officers at the Corps level. MOD is in the capital city of Kabul, so first we had the make the journey over the mountains to get there. As always a trek across the countryside of Afghanistan does not disappoint the eyes. The vistas are just incredible, especially now that we are seeing snow on the tops of the mountains.

While in the big city we stayed at one camp, and had to drive across the city to get to our meetings. This is usually no big deal for us, we simply jump into our up armored Humvees, and off we go. However, in Kabul it is "safe" enough to drive trough the city in regular trucks, so we threw on our body armor and helmets, and off we went through the city in Ford Rangers to MOD. It was by far the craziest driving I have ever experienced, and I have driven in some nutty cities. There are no lines on the streets, so lanes are merely a figment and people drive wherever there is room for their vehicles. There is also a lack of traffic laws, or at least if they do exist, they are certainly not enforced. It's pretty much an anything goes environment where you just do what you can to get where you are going. Did I include that there are no traffic lights to help control the flow of automobiles, so if you're going to dive in downtown Kabul, you must be very aggressive, or he guy behind you will ensure you know the rules with the incessant whining of his horn. I figured out that the body armor and helmets are not to protect us from any sort of enemy, but to save our lives in the event of a collision. I volunteered to drive every time, and I was glad I did. I had a great time, and I loved the rush of adrenaline as I zipped around town. Kabul is just like any other large city; there are people, cars, and buildings everywhere. Although; it is nothing like I have never seen, almost indescribable. I tried to provide as many pictures as I could of the city just to save me the task of trying to describe something I do not think I could adequately do.

Once at the meetings I got to meet all of the people involved in military communications across the country. I also go to meet the ANA Chief of Staff; he was a brilliant well-spoken man, who certainly seemed like he was in the right position. He spoke about the future of the Army, and the importance that good communications plays

in the success of that future. The Army here in Afghanistan is far more advanced that I had previously gave them credit for. Obviously I can't tell you what we discussed in the meetings, but I assure you this. Afghanistan is absolutely headed in the right direction as far as tactical communications are concerned. They have embraced the notion that technology is something they will have employ in order to be a modern army. As we all know though, technology is quite expensive, and it will be years before they are able to move into the future. It was great to establish in my mind that this Army is learning everything they possibly can from their Coalition counterparts. During every briefing it was obvious that they have success in mind, and that they strive for an independent future for Afghanistan. They also made sure that there were many thanks to the Coalition forces for helping them get to this point, and looked forward to continued success with us. It was great for me sitting there to actually hear someone say thank you for what we are doing, and that has always been the case here. The Afghan people that I have been in contact with have always thanked me for the sacrifices I have made to be here to help them. I just wanted to share that with all of you back home. The Brigadier General of Communications also invited us for a private meeting in his office that included some chi, snacks, and just some casual conversation. It was overall a really cool trip, and I was really glad I was able to be a part of it. Had I not gotten the new job, it was something I would not have experienced. It continues to prove that every dark cloud has a silver lining. Although I didn't really want to leave Khowst, the new position has already provided me opportunities to see more of this fascinating country and it's people than I anticipated. At least if I am going to forfeit my time at home to be here in Afghanistan, I am getting memories that compare to no other in exchange. I am thankful for this. I don't mean to sound so sappy, most of you know that's not really my style, must be the holiday spirit. That or it could the James Taylor I was listening to while hammering this posting out. I'll try not to let it happen again.

After a couple of great days at MOD it was time to travel back to our home up in the mountains. The snow, although very beautiful, did not do well for our return trip. It made for a pretty precarious drive, and so for the return trip we had to go around the mountains. A usual four-hour drive back to our camp turned into an over eight hour trek across the country. This trip, however, was back in my ever steadfast and safe up armored Humvee. Once again I volunteered to drive, not realizing that we wouldn't be taking a break for about six hours. May not have been the best move I have ever made, and I can't ever remember another time where my backside hurt that much. All the bumps and lack of standing vertical really took its toll. Nonetheless, we got home safe and sound, and that's all that really matters.

Now back to work. I have been spending a lot of time meeting all the new people I will be working with here, and the hardest part for me has been trying to remember everyone's name. At the Corps level there is a much bigger staff that I interact with, and I want to make sure I am respectful to them all. It is going to take me a bit of time to

learn them all, but I am sure by working with them everyday, that the names will come along. We have spent a lot of time, so far, drinking chi and talking about each other and our lives outside the military. I am sure they are doing the same thing I am, and that's trying to figure each other out, and see what makes each other tic. I have learned that trust is one thing that is very important to the people of Afghanistan, and because I am new, that trust relationship isn't there yet. As time goes on we will build that trusting relationship. For now, I'll take things as slowly as they will let me, and get to know them. We have been working on solving problems with the communications here, and they love it when we can help them solve problems. It's not that they can't solve the problems themselves; they are actually quite adept at doing that, although their solutions may be what we consider a bit unorthodox. That is what they want to learn, the conventional way of doing things, and they starve for that knowledge. It's so awesome to see the epiphany on their faces when you show them another way of doing something that may be more modern, or quicker and easier. Of course I'll keep you posted on how things are progressing.

Also I wanted to tell everyone that although last posting I really missed our shopping stores outside the camp. That loss is slowly but surely diminishing due the new store exceeding my expectations. The other day we decided to have lunch there. Now you all knew about the really good French fries, but along with those we also had some deep fat fried something that resembled hush puppies you'd get from Long John Silvers, but they tasted much better. My interpreter told me that the deep fried masses were made of potatoes, meat, and some vegetables. They continued to please later, when I didn't have any digestion issues. As you can see from the picture the ambience is awesome, but the décor has a little room for improvement. A lot of the ANA soldiers like to hang out at the "ANA Superstore", and so it's cool to meet more people as we hangout there.

Well I'm off to my next escapade, and I look forward to seeing you all very soon. For those of you who like to drop comments from time to time. You can still do that, but you must first register and then sign in from the bottom of the menu at the right of the screen.

You may have noticed the new look to the site, included in that look is some security. I made it a little harder to post comments, simply to keep the riff-raff out. I hope this doesn't cause any inconvenience, as I love the comments. Also if you were thinking of some sort of philanthropy project for the holiday season, here's your opportunity. There is a village right out side the camp here, and there are a ton of kids that live there. The children lack proper winter gear; in fact a lot of them do not even have proper shoes. If you come across some used jackets, shoes, socks, glove and hats for little dudes. I would appreciate it greatly; as it breaks my heart to see them cold, and believe me it is getting cold. The group of soldiers who live here have done humanitarian mission there before, but I think there are more kids than supplies. I thank you for considering the people here, and I know they will appreciate it a great deal. All of the school supplies that were sent to me have done the schools here wonders, and I hate to ask for more, but I feel it's the only way I can help. If this appeals to you, please drop me an email at, and I will send you my mailing address. I also want to thank everyone who has sent me a Christmas card or present, they make the holiday season a little brighter and I am grateful for it.

Sincerely,
Mark

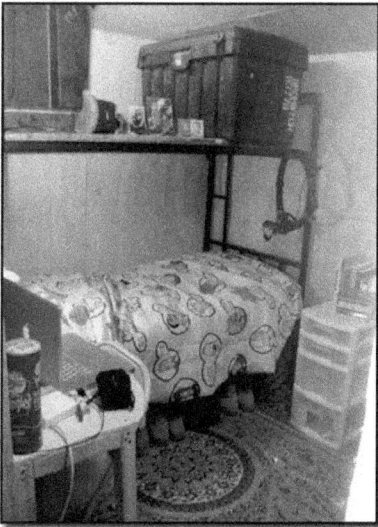

Note to self ... It is possible to live in a closet, as the picture above shows. This is my room here in Gardez. I thought you all might enjoy a glimpse into my new digs. It may not be large, but it is cozy and it will do just fine.

An Afghan Christmas Story

"I want an official Red Ryder, carbine action, two-hundred shot range model air rifle!" Ralphie

Happy Holidays all, and I hope that the season has provided everyone with warm and happy thoughts. I write this posting on Christmas day, and fortunately for us it is a white one. Last night about a foot of snow dropped from the sky, and left our camp looking just about like one of those cheesy Christmas cards you get at the day after Christmas sales. The snow has provided us with a couple of entertaining events. The first thing we decided to do was make snow angles, and so we had to find an area of snow that had not been molested by boot prints. We found our area, and promptly plopped down, and began the process of creating our heavenly beings. After the Angles came the epic snowball fight, as no first major snowfall could go without one. One cannot allow all that pristine snow to simply sit on the ground, it had to be put to use. The sun was beginning to sink below the mountains, so it wasn't easy to get a lot of people to play, but we made the most of it for those who did participate. It was awesome, and all involved had a great time. As the snow continues to fall I am sure there will be other opportunities for the icy projectiles to go flying, as I feel there is going to be an all out snow assault on each other. Well, other than the snow activities I spent my Christmas Eve and day doing my wash, getting my haircut, and cleaning my room. Just another day; kind of. Let's see what else I have been doing.

My primary counterpart has been on leave since the last time I posted, and so I haven't been able to work with him a whole lot yet. What I have been able to do, however, is spend a lot of time with the rest of his staff. It has been quite nice to get know the rest of the signal staff. My primary counterpart, Colonel Rafi, has a pretty strong personality, which causes the rest of the staff to stay somewhat dormant

with theirs. Sine he has been gone, I have really gotten to see the rest of the soldiers in the section, and more of what they are really like. They are certainly a great bunch of soldiers. Recently the Corps Signal section received a whole boatload of new signal equipment, which is great for the Corps. However, it did create quite a challenge for the soldiers of the section. What to do with it all, especially in the absence of their leader? Like I have said in earlier postings, these soldiers are the greatest of fighters, but what they lack most is the ability to logistically sustain the fight. How to properly feed, clothe, and provide other vital supplies during long term battles have certainly challenged them. With all the new radio equipment here, it is an opportunity to exercise their skills in support operations. Another characteristic that the soldiers possess that also makes it hard for them to logistically support the troops downrange is their inane need to hoard things. This trait is not unique to the Afghan army by any means; this seems to occur in all armies, at least the armies I have been involved with. Equipment always seems to be a challenge to get from higher, and so when it does finally arrive, the instinct it to keep as much of it as you can to avoid needed it again in the future. It is crucial that we get this equipment to those soldiers who are in need. As a mentor, I do not want to get too involved in the process, I would like to see the Afghan soldiers fully engaged in the actual task, and I'll simply provide advice as to how I think they are doing. They have, thus far, embraced the task of getting the equipment to the units who are in need, but they do it sparingly. Giving the units only the bare minimum needed to accomplish the task of communicating. Old habits do die hard I guess. I don't look at it as any sort of failure on their part, like I said; all Armies seem to hoard stuff, but what I do see is occasions to further mentor the troops.

Ahh ... let's see; what else has been going on. Hey, here's another first for the ANA soldiers we have been mentoring. The Afghan Commanding General decided to have a conference  for all of his leaders. Something like this is a common occurrence in the US Army, but virtually unheard of here in the ANA Army. I should first preface by saying I had nothing to do with the organization of this meeting, and really didn't do anything more than sit through it. Which was tough enough on its own, as it was an all day affair. Getting all the commanders of the lower units together in one room was a tremendous effort. They were able to take the time to report to the General how things are going, what concerns they had, and anything else that was on their minds. It was pretty cool to watch as the Kandak (Battalion) Commanders briefed the General one by one, and it was obvious it wasn't something they often do. With more practice they will certainly get better at this. The General was also able to provide the leaders of the lower units training on specific tasks, and guidance on what the future holds. As the Signal mentor of the American group, I simply listened intently when the Commanders had any concerns as pertains to their communications. This would provide me some mentoring fodder when working with my ANA section. I'm always looking for opportunities to help the section be better at what they do. My boss has said that we should mentor our ANA like we are the last mentors here in Afghanistan, and he is right. With this mindset, I try to make sure that we make the most of our time together. You never know, I could be the last mentor my section has, and I want to make sure that when I leave this place, that they are better off than when I got here. It's not all altruistic though; although I want to make sure that the ANA are in better shape when I leave, I also want to know that my time here wasn't wasted.

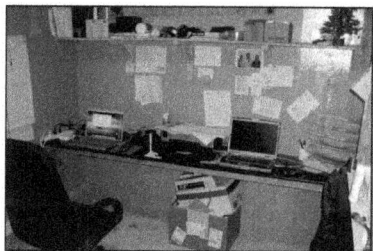

After the ANA finished the day with their Commanders

conference, we went back to our American side of the camp, and conducted a Commanders conference of our own. It was ironic that a lot of the concerns the ANA Commanders had seemed to be mirrored during our conference. Seems like both sides kind of struggle with a lot of the same issues. Maybe this is a sign of progress for the ANA. During our conference I found myself being charge of the space bar, making sure that the Power Point slides were advanced when needed. I am thinking the whole time during the meeting that I must be the highest paid space bar pusher in the world. Hey, someone's got to do it, and I have got to thank you, the tax payer, for making this all possible. Seriously, these meetings are very important. We are spread all over this country, and getting everyone together for such meetings helps us get a handle on what everyone is doing, and gets everyone the necessary information they need to conduct their missions. That's the one thing I have noticed about being at the Corps lever, versus the Brigade level I was previously at, there is no shortage of meeting. I spend a lot more time sitting at the conference table looking at Power Point slides than I used to. If you look up above, you'll see my new office, and this is where all the Power Point magic happens.

Winter, and the snow that comes with it, has definitely slowed things down around here. Time does seem to be passing a bit slower than it did during the summer, but before I know it, it will be next year. During our New Years celebration the Afghans also have another Eid holiday. It is much like the first Eid that we experienced, but this one is much shorter, only lasting three days. The timing is perfect though, because we will not lose too many days while both sides are on holiday. I know all my ANA soldiers, and my interpreter, are looking forward to the holiday. A lot of the soldiers do not go

home that frequently because of the cost, so they surely take advantage of the chance to do so when their holidays come around. The ANA General is also planning an Eid celebration here at their chow

hall, and I look forward to attending. I will certainly let you know what occurs there. Well, I am of to help serve the Christmas meal. It is tradition that the officers serve the holiday meals for the soldiers, and I look forward to it, we always make it a fun event. I want to extend a thank you to everyone who has sent me a Christmas care package, as they are really appreciated. I also want to let everyone know that if you sent any kind of food, that I have shared every bit of it with the soldiers I work with. Everyone have a safe and fun Holiday Season, and I will chat again with you soon. Talk to you next year.

Sincerely,
Mark

PS ... "No way kid, you'll shoot your eye out" Santa

Bromwich's Shiny New Year

"Always in motion is the future" Yoda

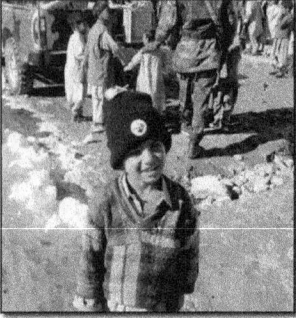

Welcome back everyone. I hope that the passing from last year into this fresh shiny new one met all of you with happy hearts and minds. The passing of each year always reminds me that I am about to become a year older, and that I need to make sure I take that retrospective look back to ensure that I have done alright for the year. It also reminds me that I am getting further and further away from being cool, and that gravity can do some awful things to the human body. The past year, in my estimation, has been an excellent year. I have done a lot more than I ever anticipated doing, that's for sure, and for a majority of the time it has been quite positive. Working here in Afghanistan has provided me with the opportunity to have such a brilliant year, and I am rather pleased that I was given this mission. I believe that I have made a difference here thus far, and I also believe that I will continue to make a difference here until I return home. Ahh … my resolution for the year. Good question. I will resolve to get home safely, and resume my life with family and friends. It's simple, but it works. That and if I decided to make the usual life altering resolution, like work on

my memory skills, I am sure to forget about it by February or March. Anyhow … Here's the part in our broadcast where we bring you up to date with what's been going on.

Here in Afghanistan it has been celebrations all around. During our holiday celebrations from Christmas to New Years, we have been enjoying gathering together to eat special meals and the company of each other. On New Years Eve we stayed up until midnight to watch the clock click past twelve. We were hoping for some fireworks, but the folks from our security force didn't have enough explosives to waste on that particular night to give us a show. That's all right though, it is better that we save them in the event that we really need them. It would be a tough one to explain to the bosses, why we weren't able to defend ourselves, because we blew our explosives for a New Years Eve show. Opps. During our New Years celebration, peoples of the Muslim faith were also celebrating a holiday. They were observing another Eid holiday, called Eid Al-Adha, or the Celebration of Sacrifice. This particular Eid starts around January 30th, and goes until around the 1st of January. The reason for the arounds, is that the Muslims use a solar calendar, as opposed to the US. We use a lunar calendar, so the days do not always line up exactly the same. The three days is to celebrate the sacrifice the Prophet Abraham made when God asked him to kill one of his sons. Thankfully, the story has a happy ending. Instead of Abraham killing his son, as he was just about to do, God asked him to stop and kill a goat instead. Well, the story is kind of happy, except for the goat that is, but it showed the incredible devotion Abraham had for God. The Muslim people celebrate this sacrifice and devotion with great meals, and then when the family has ended the meal, they are to give whatever is left to poor families that cannot afford such meals. It is again, like the last Eid, a time for families to spend time with each other, sometimes they may give gifts, and then often they visit distant family and friends. As I was speaking to my ANA counterparts, they asked me all about Christmas, and how a typical American family may celebrate this holiday. As I was explaining Christmas, I queried them all about the Eid, and how it is celebrated. We both came to discover that we are very similar in the way we celebrate such religious holidays. It was a cool moment for both parties, knowing that although our religions and cultures may be much different, really when you get down to the core of things, we are really quite similar. Family and friends are very important, and that giving gifts to each other, or feeding the poor, is something that we both thought were fundamental during the holiday seasons.

Most of the ANA soldiers went home during the Eid celebration to be home with family, but for the ANA soldiers that stayed behind, the American forces got some money together, and hired a local band for them. It was a lot of fun to watch the ANA soldiers get down to the tunes that the

band was belting out. I didn't understand a word of the lyrics, and the music itself was pretty alien, but the ANA soldiers seem to enjoy it very much. Once again, although very different, the dancing was very similar to the way we dance. There was some freestyle action going on, where the soldiers would just go all out, and moved rhythmically to the way the music made them feel. Then there were some dances that were very structured, a lot like country line dancing, where they followed a much prescribed number of dance steps. I decided not to get involved in the dancing, as I am not a very good dancer to begin with, and it was their celebration. The only odd thing about it all was that because we were on a military installation, there were no women dancing, so it was just an all out man dance. Little different than we are used to, and from what I understand, not unusual for only men to dance at celebrations even in their civilian worlds. All in all, all the holiday celebrations were a lot of fun, and I learned even more about my ANA brethren.

Yesterday was a great day for me. I got to go on a humanitarian mission to a small village outside of Gardez called Robat. It was my first humanitarian mission since being here in

Gardez, and I was just ecstatic about the whole thing. The drive out to the village wasn't too long, but I was the turret gunner in our Humvee, so I was about a degree away from being a Popsicle by the time we got there. As soon as we arrived at the edge of the village a few children

spotted our convoy, and they immediately went about the task of alerting the rest of the children to our arrival. We do not tell the people of the village we are coming, and that's for obvious security reasons. However, whenever we roll into a village like we did, and the children see four trucks overloaded giant white boxes, they can almost guess we are there to see them specifically. Especially this little village, as it was nestled right up against the bottom of some huge mountains, and there really isn't a thru street onto any other place in Afghanistan. We were there for them, and these little dudes knew it. Immediately I was glad that this village was chosen, because I saw children without proper shoes or jackets, and it was too cold to be without either. Some of the guys commented on the state of the village, and how it had improved so much since they first started going there. When they started delivering supplies to this village most of the people lived in tents, and now there were mud homes with doors and windows where the tents once stood. The villagers have decided to make this their permanent home, and as you can see from the pictures, it is a cute little village. Although cute, the people who live there are definitely poor, and there was no escaping that they did need our help.

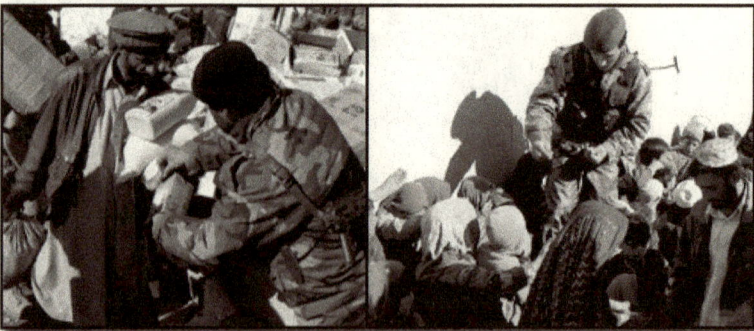

As soon as we stopped the trucks the ANA soldiers immediately started to unload the trucks onto the main street of the village. We want the ANA soldiers to be the ones to give out the supplies to the villagers. Although a vast majority of the supplies came from the US, we encourage the ANA to be responsible for its delivery. We encourage the ANA to be the ones to deliver the supplies because then the people of Afghanistan see that it is their Army that is providing them the things they need. It is a campaign to help build confidence in the new Afghan Army, and it also builds that same confidence in their new government. It is the hope of the US Army that programs such as this will provide a stronger influence on the people of Afghanistan. If the citizens see their government willing to help and protect them, they will not have to rely on terrorist or warlords for the very same things. So, after everything was piled up on the main street, the soldiers lined up the citizens of this little village, and handed out food, cooking oil, tea, and anything else the people could carry. It was awesome to see the expressions on their faces, although we had the language barrier, one cannot mistake the look on their faces. They were more than appreciative of what they had received. After the food supplies were handed out, the soldiers went to work on getting shoes, jackets, gloves, and hats to the children who needed them. During this time the boxes that held the toys and candy were also broken out. Children were happy everywhere I looked. It was tough for them to decide what they wanted more, toys, candy, or clothing. As more of the clothing, toys, and candy made their way to the surface of the pile, the ANA pretty much lost control at this point.

It became a mass of controlled chaos, and the spectacle was fun to watch. I am sure we would not have done that much better, and truly, the ANA did a great job with everything on this mission. During the mission I spent my time interacting with the children. I would try and talk to them as much as possible, but we didn't bring enough interpreters, so a lot of the communication occurred through hand motions. I still had a fabulous time playing with them, and we even had an impromptu snowball fight. During bouts of snowballs and having fun with the kids, I would seek out the more timid one, and help them wrestle their way up to the front of the line to get something they needed. I wanted to make sure everyone got a chance to get

something. After the few hours I was ready to head back to camp, the cold and weight of my gear had taken its toll. Plus everything

we brought was now in the hands of those who needed it. As we drove off I couldn't help but think about what will become of the people of this village. Will they ever...

Sometimes I wish we had more stuff to give out, especially the necessities like food. We are fortunate to have as much stuff as we did, and there are a lot of people to thank. I want to make sure that I do thank those who have helped me collect the ninety-two boxes of supplies I have added to our efforts here. The first is my sons' school, the Malcolm Price Laboratory School. His class, and the entire Share and Care Carnival sent so many wonderful items to help our cause. Usually they collect foodstuffs for the local food bank, but this year decided the cause here in Afghanistan was an imperative. I Thank You. Angie and her Church from Wisconsin, the ever-steadfast contributors. You guys have helped keep the children here warm during he coldest parts of the year. I also Thank You. My other great friend Angie and all her students at the High School in Brooklyn, thank you for keeping the schools open here. Agnieszka, I thank you for sending so many brilliant items, and for keeping the entertainment quotient high in a pace that could surely use it. Everyone, this is going to be a great year, and I look forward to it. This is the year I get to come home; my role in this mission will be complete, and I look forward to our next conversation.

Sincerely,
Mark

The Eloquent President: A Visit From Karzai

"And then I had to see the President . . . Again?" Gump

Hello everyone and I hope that you are all in good spirits. It has been a long last couple of weeks for me. I have been battling germs lately, and sadly my body lost the clash of microbes within, so I succumbed to a wicked cold. I got all the classic symptoms of the common variety cold that the Vicks folks talk about in their commercials, and they were pretty intense. Everything here is so extreme, and colds are not excluded from this category. It was simply miserable. Not to worry though, our fine medics here have a fully stocked pharmacy of the good stuff, and weren't afraid to dole it out. After a couple of days of suffering, I was back to feeling pretty normal. Along with the torment of my Afghan cold, I also broke a tooth, and I broke it pretty good. Back home this is not normally an issue, but here the dentist is quite a ride away, and we do not make the trip everyday. So I have had to wait a few days before I can catch a ride up north to see the dentist. Thankfully it is just a broken tooth, and not some sort of painful root infection. If it were a painful break, the wait could have really sucked, and I would definitely found my way back to the fully stocked pharmacy for some relief.

Miserable cold and broken tooth aside; things here are still pretty cool. We are inching ever so close to having our very own coffee shop. That's right … I said coffee shop. Who would have thought that in the middle of a war zone, one could take a break from the war to enjoy a hot freshly brewed cappuccino from a trained barista? Now that's what I am talking about, no more brown colored swill from the chow hall, but real coffee. The workers are toiling day and night to get the shop off the ground. It may not look like much now, but when it is complete, it will be like

sipping a cup of brew at a Parisian sidewalk cafe. Well, maybe not that first rate, but at least it will be better than the stuff we make. Another creature comfort we are having installed in our camp here is the Internet. It will be a lot like we had in Khowst, where the connection is right in our sleeping quarters. I will no longer have to trudge through the snow to get online; I can stay in the comfort of my closet, and webcam home. We are all quite excited about this addition to our little slice of heaven.

Top story of the week: President Karzai visits Khowst. That's right, the President of Afghanistan dropped in for the grand opening of the

new ANA camp down at Khowst. I preface this part of the post by saying that I wasn't able to go to Khowst for the official grand opening. With all the dignitaries involved, there wasn't enough room for a lowly Captain on the flight down, and there wasn't a planned ground movement either. I was pretty sad about this. While I was down in Khowst, we did a lot of work to get the new ANA camp where it is today. Working with the ANA staff to move in and prepare the new facility for operations, and it would have been nice to see the final episode from that portion of my deployment. I did get some pictures from my friends from South Dakota though, so it's all-good. From what heard, due to inclement weather, the visit from the President had to be cut short, or the helicopters would have been grounded. Having the President show up was a pretty big deal, as President Karzai rarely leaves the capital city, for obvious security reasons, so it was great that he felt the camp opening was important enough to attend. Now the installation is officially up and running and I believe they decided to call it Camp Parsa. It is named after a famous Mujahdeen warrior during the time of the Soviet invasion. The camp, and the ANA soldiers who reside there, are a significant step toward

the securing and stabilizing the area of Khowst, and I am really happy to have played a really small part in helping this occur.

Let's see … what else is new. Well, a couple of days ago we had a change of command ceremony for the American side. Our previous Commander is on his way home now, and so we now have a new Colonel running the show here. What made our change of command ceremony different from any other one I have seen in the past was that we had the ANA General get involved in the formal procedure. The General of the ANA Corps oversaw the traditional passing of the flags. It is a ritual where the outgoing Commander of a unit ceremoniously passes on the flag, or unit colors, onto the incoming Commander. The ANA General was honored to be a part of the ceremony, and he was the first Afghan soldier in Afghanistan to take part in such proceedings. I thought it was grand to have the ANA involved, especially since they are the reason we are here. The commander of our unit is also his mentor. It was cool that he had a hand in presenting command to his new mentor. Our new Colonel is a pretty good guy; it should be a lot of fun working for and with him.

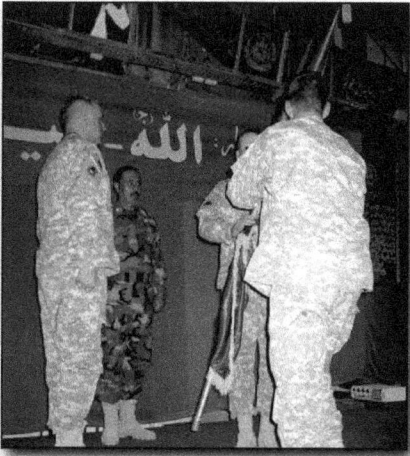

Because of the cold weather, which has lowered the some of enemies' activities, we have had time to do some practical training for the ANA. We are currently working on what is called a CPX, or Command Post Exercise. The idea is we have created a training session where the ANA staff has to react to different kinds of scenarios, and they are rated on how they perform. What we are mostly looking for is how well they communicate with each other, and how well the use decision making processes to deal with the situation when one of these scenarios occurs. The scenarios are all sorts of simulated events that could occur during a real battle, and then everything the ANA do is tracked by evaluators to be assessed later on. It is the first time the Corps ANA are going to be involved in a CPX, and it should prove to be a lot of fun, and I'll bet at times, a lot of heartache. The whole exercise will run for forty-eight hours, and I get the feeling sometimes I will be there for the whole time. I still look forward to the training exercise though, and it will be good for the ANA to take part in.

Four days later ...The ANA have completed the CPX, and for the most part it was successful. There were a few bumps in the road, but they were totally expected, as this was their first attempt at a CPX. They did a great job of responding to the scenarios that we threw at them, and they communicated well between the sections. These were the areas that we were assessing, and their marks were pretty high. Some of the problems that occurred fell directly on me, and my ANA G6 counterpart, so we will have some work to do to better prepare this Corps for operations. One of our concerns is computer training. The Afghans do not get a lot of computer use, and it definitely showed itself during the CPX, when they tried to use them. The ANA G6, and I, has decided to beef up our computer-training program to help the soldiers become more comfortable with the machines. We actually expected the problems with lack of experience, and were quite glad that the difficulty surfaced. This will help stress how important it is for the soldiers to attend computer training. Another drawback to the computer use that we noticed was a translation issue. The computers that the ANA use have a Standard English installation of the XP operating system, and this caused some of the users to struggle with usage of their workstations. Thankfully, the solution to this problem is simple; Microsoft has Farsi language support for the operating system. Farsi is pretty close to Dari and Pashto, the language that a majority of the soldiers speak. The only problem is getting all that machines to the technicians, so they can add the support package to the computers. This is a logistical challenge that we will tackle right after the weekend. After the CPX the ANA and the US conducted an AAR, which is an after action review. This is where both sides take the time to sit down together, and analyze how the whole event went. Both sides were quite glad to be complete, and all the tired bloodshot eyes in the crowd truly expressed this sentiment. Each of the heads of the sections took the time to express what they did well in, and what they need to improve. It was nice to hear that the sections embraced the training, took away from the training good lessons, and the AAR didn't become a blame-fest. Once each of the sections were allowed their confessional, the ANA Corps Commander took the floor, he praised his troops for the good exercise, and then made mention that we should do this again in a couple of months. Oh Boy … I can't wait.

Honestly it has been a good last couple of week, very busy, but overall very good. I like being busy; it really helps the passing of time. We are about

four and a half months from being done with our tour already. I didn't think time would go fast, but you know how vacations go, the time just passes you by. It been a while since I have updated you on how many steak days are left, so here goes, there are only twenty of them left. Sweet. I can't wait until my last steak day; it will be quite a celebration. To add, I am only about a month away from my leave, and I so look forward to getting on the plane for that trip. Soon enough. I also want to thank everyone who has continued to support me while I have been here, and the immense support I have received for my humanitarian aid campaign. All the stuff sent has been, at times, overwhelming, and so appreciated. When I first started the drive, my goal was to get a few things to give to the schools, and that has since branched out to so much more, and I do not have anyone to thank but all of you who got involved. It has been very rewarding to help the Afghan Army move towards autonomy, but when I include what we have been able to do for the citizens of Afghanistan, it's to the point where it's indescribable. Thank You and I will talk to you again soon.

Sincerely,
Mark

Saw the picture of the bicycle as I was going through the images of the CPX, which were taken by someone else, and thought I would show everyone what a jingled up bike looks like. Also, the pictures of President Karzai were taken by another photographer as well, so I thought I make sure I give credit where credit is due. The only problem is I shouldn't put names on here, so that's as close as I can get.

The Wobbling Oddball: A Redundant Story from Bromwich

"Sometimes you can observe a lot just by watching." Berra

Welcome back everyone. I'll bet given that it has been so long since my posting, you all thought I wasn't going to come back. Well, here I am back at it, just kind of lost track of time. We have just been so awfully busy lately; I hadn't taken the time to sit down a write a few lines about what I am up to. I have heard that in Iowa the weather has been absolutely miserable, temperatures below what any living creature should withstand, and I am sorry to hear that. Here in Afghanistan, besides the occasional snowfall, it has been beautiful. The temperatures have been certainly tolerable, and I haven't worn a jacket in weeks. Sorry to brag, but it's the only thing I got over on you guys at home, so I thought I'd rub it in a bit. Another positive item for you all, as you can see from the picture below, it depicts me enjoying a grilled cheese sandwich, along with some tomato soup. It is quite possibly the world's most perfect meal. It has taken months to convince our cooking staff here that these two items belong together, and really should never be served apart. Since the time I have arrived in Gardez, we would have grilled cheese sandwiches, but no tomato soup, and vice versa. Well one day the planets aligned, cats and dogs played together, and the grilled cheese sandwiches were served with tomato soup. I thought this must be some kind of trick, had the cooking staff finally taken to our advice? Yes, just that one day, as we have not had the two served together since. It was just one of those days, like catching a solar eclipse, or seeing a fully arced rainbow; you take the time to enjoy it, because you may never see it again. I did remember to photograph it, because I knew that the moment wouldn't last forever, but images would. That and I wasn't sure anyone would believe me when I tell them it actually happened one day, here at Camp Lightning.

I actually just returned from a trip to the Capital city of Kabul, it was a great time, kind of like a little mini vacation away from this place. I was on the mission to help get some of the soldiers from our area to the Capital city, as they were on their way home for good. It was a bit bitter sweet though. Although I was quite happy knowing my friends was to be going home, at the same time I was quite envious, and wanted to go with them. Knowing that they would be back in the US within a couple of days, and I would not, made it hard to smile with them as we sat in the coffee shop trading stories of our deployment. I had worked with some of the guys for moths, and got used to having them around. They were all a bunch of exceptional soldiers, and I will miss my new friends. It was okay though, they had all spent a year here, and it was their turn to go home. I knew that my group is the next to go through

the same thing, and I am sure the people who drive us to the airport will feel the same way as I did. The nice thing was I got to spend some last moments with them before they took off, which the people back in Gardez missed out on. We spent one night at the coffee shop, where they were having a Karaoke competition. Minus the beer, it was much like what we do at home. Some were rather good at the singing thing, while other, not so much. It was the others crowd that gave us the really good entertainment. We sat back, and sipped hot mocha lattes, and laughed heartily at those who didn't sing so well, but kind of thought they did. For a moment there, it was almost like we weren't in uniform, and in the middle of a war zone. I forgot about everything here for a few brief, and pleasurable, minutes. I really enjoyed my friends, as if we were at a local bar, enjoying the not so good group of singers. It is a moment I will truly remember for a long time. I already miss my friends, and I wish them well as they try to assimilate back into their normal worlds. I will tell you, if any of you guys are out there reading this, the drive back to Gardez was lonely without you. Good luck with all you do. Right after I returned to lovely Camp Lightning, I hopped right back into an Armored Humvee the very next day. I was off to see the Governor of Gardez. He happened to be hosting a meeting, I wasn't sure what type yet, but it seemed like an opportunity not to miss. In order to go to the meeting I had to make myself seem useful, so I took the gun turret, and then it seemed like I

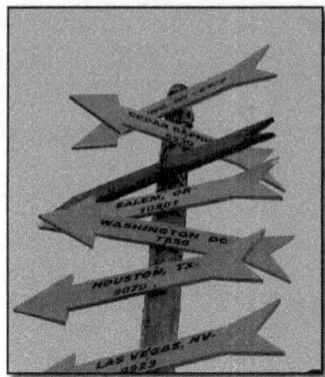

was needed for the trip. Otherwise, I may not have had a need to go. I may have wanted to think the whole thing through a bit. Remember when I told you it's been nice around here, except for the occasional snow. Well this day was one of those occasional times, and it was freaking cold. I bundled up as best I could, and off we went to see the Governor. It was actually a good bit of serendipity, as the meeting was really cool; there were a ton of elders, local politicians, Mullahs, and public officers. They were all discussing the economic and industrial development of the Gardez area. I didn't have my trusty interpreter with me, so some of the details are a bit sketchy, but just sitting in the audience among these community leaders was quite an honor. We tried to strike up a conversation with the Governors private police, and from I was able to piece together, they really liked my uniform. I mean really liked it and I am sure if I had agreed, the guy would have gone home with it on. Due to the cold, and not to mention the awkwardness of running around in my jockeys, I wasn't able oblige the officer.

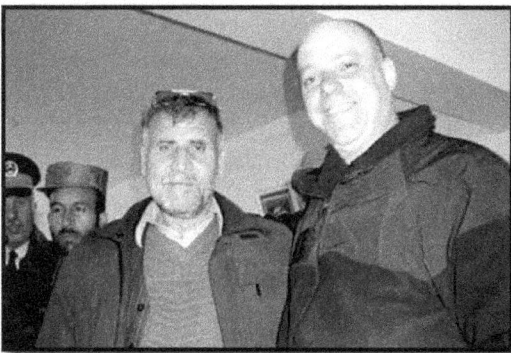

Nonetheless, they were pretty good guys, and they made sure to thank us for what we do.

Part of the discussion was also talk about how the US Army will be training the Afghan Police force now. It has just recently become part of our mission here in Afghanistan, along with continued support for the Afghan Army. Thankfully I am not part of the training team; I am probably not the best role model for the police. Maybe it was my extended stay in my college fraternity, but I have spent more time on the other side of the law, and therefore maybe not the best example to model. Actually, the US has decided to take people who have real police training, which makes the most sense to me, and the National Guard soldiers have a lot of people who are peace officers back home. It will be a much better source of training than me. I think it will be a cool part of our mission, and also lend itself to getting Afghanistan even closer to the point where they will no longer need us. After the meeting was completed we went to the Governors mansion for lunch. As you can see form the picture below, I was pretty focused on my meal. It was a traditional lunch of rice, and in the rice are carrots, raisins, and meat. The meal tasted fantastic, and we had a blast hanging out with the governor and about fifty of his other closest friends. On this trip I also took along my Communications Sergeant, because up until now he hadn't been allowed to go on a trip such as this. I thought it is about time he get out of the office for a bit, and gather some other memories. He was so amped up, he couldn't stop

talking about his experiences, and I was happy he was able to come along. I would hate for him to leave this country with only the memories of working in our office, and maybe a couple of convoys to go on pass and leave. This place is so different from anything we have ever experienced in the United States, it would be such a waste to travel thousands of miles, and not really witness any of it.

Ahh … so what else is going on around here? Well, I am back in the classroom, teaching computer applications to the ANA here at the Corps, but with a slight twist. The courses the Afghan soldiers are taking are designed purely for the communications soldiers who are already pretty proficient with the machines, and the idea is that they will be the next set of trainers for the Corps. After the CPX, we learned that the soldiers in the Corps could use some help working with their computers, but instead of me teaching the courses to the Corps, we decided to make trainers out of communications soldiers. I am teaching the Microsoft software suite again, but it is really as a refresher, so I am including all types of teaching strategies for them along the way. It is fun to watch them go through this process, because it is so new for them. They are so used to being trained by us, and now they will be responsible for their own training. I give them opportunities to get in front of the class, and you I can tell that some of them get pretty nervous. I think after they have taught the curriculum a few times, they will get the hang of it. It is a big step though, and it is what we continue to strive for, and that is they being independent. This is that step towards that self-reliance, and once again they have been very receptive to the training. I

think my Afghan communications brothers will make great trainers, and I look forward to sitting through a couple of their courses to witness their success.

Speaking of training. Our camp here has been over run by new recruits. The National Training Center in Afghanistan has run out of room, due to the high number of soldiers wanting to join the Army. In response to this over crowding, they have opened the gates to our camp to the newly recruited soldiers, and they will now to their initial basic training here. There are new Afghan dudes everywhere, and they all seem like the happiest bunch of men I have seen. Every time I drive by none of them can hold their smile in, and several of the guys shout

a hello to me. It is awesome to see all these young Afghan men want to be part of defending their nation. There must be at least a thousand of these guys running around the camp. They are involved with all types of training, like marching, saluting, and other basic military skills. Later they will also be involved in more difficult military training like rifle marksmanship, land navigations, and personal hygiene. Not kidding about that last one. A lot of these soldiers are coming from a very rural background, and so they will lack a lot of the skills we think should be inherent. They will also be taking classes on literacy, and other social skills that they may not have received while growing up in rustic Afghanistan. Another program we are trying to implement here at the Corps is a vocational training school for the soldiers. Once they are full fledged soldiers, who have graduated from their training, they can even get involved in courses taught here at the camp that will provide them a vocation skill, such as plumbing or electrical wiring. If the soldier decides to leave the army when his enlistment is up, he will at least have a tangible skill that they can use to earn a living. I think it is a brilliant program, and I look to get involved in any way I can.

Well, as you can see, it has been quite busy around here, and there have been a lot of neat changes going on. It also seems as if I have told some of this story already. Weird, but maybe I am having a giant Afghan Deja Vu, like we all have been here before. Anyhow, I apologize for blabbing on and on, but it's been so long, and I had a lot to say. Well, here I go again, time to blab some more. To all who have aided in the humanitarian aid, we have together, collected over one hundred boxes of supplies. That is incredible, and twice the goal I set when I first put the little blurb about collecting stuff in this blog. Who would have thought it would have gone this far, and as usual I have no one to thank but all of you for helping me, and the people of Afghanistan. The awesome thing is there are more boxes on the way, and maybe we can hit one hundred and fifty boxes of supplies, that would be awesome, and totally achievable. I am so glad that this deployment has given me an opportunity to do so much more than a typical deployment. When I first received the call to action, I never even fathomed that my experiences would be so vast and significant. I would also to put in a special thank you to Ginny, your coat drive was unbelievable, and I can not wait until the article is published. You should all be very pleased with the success, and I hope the article reflects that. I can't believe that this journey is coming close to end. I will be going on leave within a week or so, and I will go for about a month. When I return from leave, I will have a mere sixty days left here. I think after my last days, it will time. Time to come home, time to let others take my place, and time to get back to what I consider my normal life. This vacation has been fantastic, but with all good things, they must come to end. Talk to all real soon, and for some of you, I'll see you real soon. Again I thank all of you who have done anything to make this deployment remarkable.

Sincerely,
Mark

This picture was taken on our way to Kabul. I couldn't resist taking the picture of the frost on the trees; at times it didn't look real. It was like someone had used that fake snowy Christmas tree spray stuff. This place never ceases to surprise me with moments like this.

I Only Rest Between the Deep Breaths

"I still need more healthy rest in order to work at my best. My health is the main capital I have and I want to administer it intelligently."
Hemingway

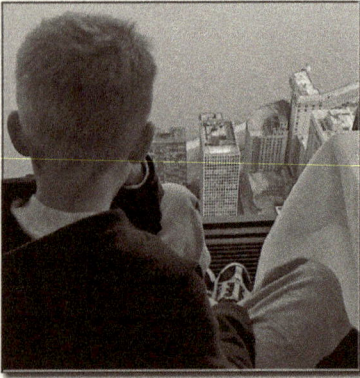

Over a forty-eight hour span I spent in excess of twenty hours in an airplane, about seven hours waiting for various airplanes, and the rest of the time trying to get some sleep. It was all in an attempt to get home for my two weeks of Rest and Relaxation. The outcome; I made it home, quite tired, but I made it. When I arrived at the airport in Cedar Rapids, Iowa, I hardly noticed my children. A lot has changed with them physically over the last nine months. It was incredible to see those immediately noticeable changes in them, and that's when it hit me, I had been gone a long time. The time in Afghanistan didn't seem all that long, at least not nine months worth, but obviously it was

passing on, and with young children those changes are dramatic. The reunion was one of the most emotional times of my life, more so than when ET escaped on the flying bicycle. Thankfully I didn't turn into a blubbering crybaby, although quite tempting, but there was way too

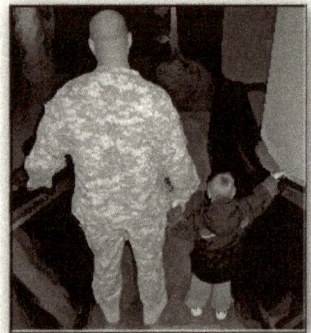

much of an audience for that. However, there were other people in the airport that we didn't know, who had started to cry. It was quite a scene. I was glad to know that other people, who aren't in the military, got to eyewitness how much we sacrifice to do what we do.

Once home, I had an agenda, and that was to make sure I made as much contact as I possibly could with friends and family. I had a great time reuniting with everyone, and I hope that the time was enough. If I failed to include anyone, my apologies, it certainly wasn't intentional. There were three items that I observed when I met up with everyone. The first one; time and distance do little to affect good relationships. When I spoke with everybody at get-togethers, it was if we had only been apart for a very short while. It was really astonishing to notice that, really, little effort was required to reconnect with my family, friends, and colleagues. The second thing; people really appreciate what we have been doing here, and this one is for everyone I met during my travels. Although they may not have been of the same political persuasion, or appreciated the war, that didn't seem matter. What mattered was that they were proud of the work we were doing, and that we were serving our country as best we could. For those who I met along the way, I thank you for your generosity. I don't think I paid for a whole lot while moving through the various airports. It always seemed that there was someone there who would pick up my tab, without even knowing me, or me knowing about it, because they wanted to do something more to say thanks. For those who did just say thanks for the service, you are appreciated just as well, and you're all welcomed. The last thing I noticed was after over nine months without any sort of libations, I had become the world's cheapest date. It did not take long to notice the effects of a well-poured Guinness, and the mornings after consequences if I had asked for one too many. It figures that I would get to participate in the war that is alcohol free, certainly not like the days of old, but overall I think it is a good choice. This place is depressing enough on its own; we definitely don't need to add a depressant to the mix.

Well after a few days of being at home, it was time to move onto the vacation phase of the trip home. The family, and I, decided to have some alone time, so off we went to spend six days in Chicago. My family absolutely loves Chicago, especially the boys. The big draw for them is them is the Shedd's Aquarium, Sears and Hancock tower, and the Field Museum. My boys decided that the first day there that we would visit the "big buildings", which are the Sears and Hancock. They love to go up to the observations decks, and look out

over the city. My eldest son had been saving his money, because he wanted to do something special for me while we were in Chicago. He set his mind on buying me lunch for my birthday at the restaurant on the top of the

Hancock tower. It was pretty awesome, the food was great, and what an immense gesture from a seven year old. However, I ended up paying the tab; I think his money is better served going into the bank for something later. Don't tell him though. The views were absolutely spectacular, and above are a couple of pictures from our table. The next day we went to Shedd's Aquarium. My three year old loved the dolphin show, but was convinced that the

dolphins were not real, but that they were in fact actually robots. It explained how the humans were able to get them to do the tricks, and you never know, he could be right. Then off to the Field Museum, and the first thing we saw when we entered the main hall was Sue the T-Rex. After minutes of intense study of the dinosaurs' remains, I came up with a theory to explain their extinction. You see; the short arms didn't allow for dino-tooth brushing, and therefore they died out do to cavities and gingivitis. One cannot expect to be a mega scary carnivore without sharp dinosaur teeth. At least that's what I told my kids to encourage proper dental hygiene. My eldest son immediately corrected me, letting me know that the latest theory for dinosaur extinction is that a giant meteorite may have struck the earth. Oh, darn smart school … I like my idea better. I could go on and on about our trip to Chicago, but I do not want to bore anyone with the details. I don't think there us anything worse than being forced to look at someone's vacations pictures.

Staying on the thirty-fifth floor of the Marriot in Chicago, on the "Magnificent Mile" no less, is certainly not cheap, so we found some employment for the boys to help offset the costs we were accruing while staying there. I would have been there to help, but I'm not so good with the whole heights thing. Darn vertigo.

Well, anyhow, my time home was well spent, and I definitely had a good time. I really wasn't looking forward to the trip back, but of course as all good things, they must come to an end. Off to the airport I go to endure the massive amount of traveling it takes to move halfway around the globe, back to Afghanistan. I look forward to

 getting back though, believe it or not, because when I return we only have about sixty days left before our tour is complete. Getting back to Afghanistan means the countdown on those last days begins. I just cannot

wait to put this whole deployment away on the shelves of my long-term memory. I really believe that we are doing good things there, and that our time and efforts are truly appreciated, but being home for two weeks has reminded me that I have another place I really need to be, other than Afghanistan. I also want to make sure that I thank the students, teachers, and staff of the Malcolm Price Laboratory School. You were all so awesome when I stopped in to see you, and your continued support of our humanitarian efforts is immensely appreciated.

Sincerely,
Mark

This post has been dedicated to the ever steadfast, and endearing, Ruth Erickson, my wife's grandmother. I am truly appreciative of the many years that we were able to know each other, and will forever miss you, now that you have passed onto the next realm.

One, Two, Three ... More Stars for the Constellation

" You can't steal stuff, that will get you in trouble, but you can steal knowledge." Ali

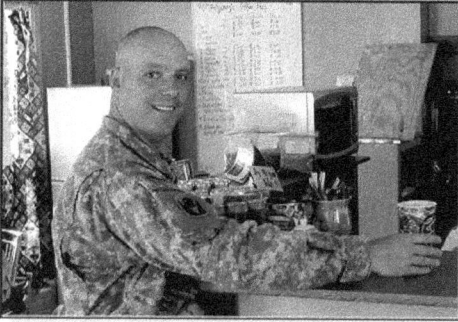

Welcome back everyone and I hope you are all in good health and spirits. Well, I have been back for a little over week now, and everything has been pretty good so far. There were a couple of things that have occurred while I was away, and the most important one is our coffee shop has been completed, and is now open for business. No more drinking what our cafeteria folk's calls coffee, and no more hoping for donations of beans while I frantically search through mail from home. That's right, whenever I start to feel the symptoms of caffeine withdrawal; I can walk right over to our new café, and order any of the caffeine-laden concoctions without hesitation. The only downside to having our newly christened café is that they do not give the coffee away, so I am going to require our finance team to stop by our camp more often, as I seem to spending all my allowance at the coffee shop. Thankfully we don't have an ATM here on camp, as Shelly and I would have to change our lifestyle a bit to support my habit.

Another transformation that has been occurring while I was away is the weather, and all that goes with the spring season here in Afghanistan. The snow, ice, and miserable cold, have thankfully ceded too much nicer temperatures. Our little chunk of Afghanistan is showing signs of life again, and we are seeing the return of green foliage on the few trees that live in our area. The farmers in the area are frantically at work trying to divert what melted snow water they can from the streams and rivers into their fields. Beginning the process of flood irrigation and this process should continue until all the snow has melted from the mountaintops. Hopefully this spring will bring enough of the rains needed to continue a good growing season for them. The new greenery has also brought back the nomadic tribe, the Kuchies, allowing their herds of sheep, goats, or camels, feed in the cooler temperatures of the high mountains. In my earlier posting, while still in Khowst, as the weather started to turn cold, they all moved down there to keep their herds in warmer weather. It is kind of cool to be higher up in the mountains to see their return. It also sort of brings my tour here in Afghanistan a full circle. It is a sign that we are soon to be out of here, and back home. I can't wait. Although the time here has been like nothing I have ever experienced in my life, it is time to close the pages on this chapter of my life, and continue writing the chapters of the life I have in the US.

Only a couple days had passed since my return here to Gardez, and I had to jump right into action. We were expecting a visit from some dignitaries from the Ministry of Defense (MOD). The guy in charge of all Afghan Army communications, General Ali, felt that he needed to visit with COL Rafi and the communications section here at Gardez. Why not, it's a good a time as any to drop in. The only concern we had, was we were left with a really short planning time. We wanted to make sure that the Generals visit was worth his while, so after some intense meeting time with COL Rafi, we had a plan in place. The next day as we were preparing our Humvees, doing some last minute checks, my cell phone rings. It was the General, and his

American mentors, they were patiently awaiting our arrival to the Gardez airport. This is not good. We didn't even start the visit, and we already somehow missed our first time hack. Well ... that's kind of embarrassing, but none the less off we went. This was COL Rafi's first time in a Humvee, and at my high rate of speed over the rough roads of Afghanistan, I am pretty sure it may be his last. I doubt he'll ever want to ride with me again, but you gotta fly when you're late. Once we got to the airport, we found out that we weren't really late, but the plane had left way ahead of schedule. Whew, crisis averted. We then drove over to the ANA camp, and a luncheon had been prepared for us, it was a very nice meal with good conversation. Thanks to our interpreters. I haven't really learned as much of the language as I imagined I would by now, the interpreters make it easy not to try hard enough. We gave the General, and the other VIP's a tour of our ANA communications facilities, and they all seemed quite impressed with our set-up. It was a nice end to day one of their visit.

The next day we held a Signal Symposium of sorts. We gathered about forty Signal soldiers from all over our area of operations,

and they were afforded the opportunity to address any issues they had with the current status of communications within their particular organizations. The meeting went really well, and all the soldiers' comments were well received by GEN Ali. The General spoke with a calm and quiet voice, as he provided guidance to his troops. It was obvious that the soldiers had a respect for this man, and not simply because he was an Army General, but more because he spoke to the soldiers, instead of at them. This is the first time I had been able to witness something like this in Afghan Army, and it was really

refreshing to see. I hope it a trend they will continue long after we are all gone. Sometimes higher officers, such as Generals, can get somewhat removed from the issues that plague soldiers at the lower levels. It is not unusual in any Army, but General Ali seemed pretty genuine about taking care of his soldiers, and it also demonstrated to the lower soldiers that they do have a voice, and that their thoughts matter, a concept truly new for the Army of Afghanistan. So, day two is put down into the books as a success.

Somehow I knew the trend couldn't continue, and day three proved that assumption. The last day of the visit, before we had to head back to the Gardez airport, we sat down with all the senior leadership of the communications. General Ali wanted to provide us with an overview of his thoughts from the past two days, and other pearls of wisdom he'd been holding onto for this visit. That's when he let us have it. He didn't yell or scream, but this is when his calm voice had that disappointed father tone. I hate that, it is worse than being yelled at. He let us know that we were not providing the enough training to the soldiers down range, that we had to make sure they could do their jobs. The big hit, computer training, and he is right, we have not been getting the computer training down to the lower levels. We have been so focused with trying to make sure the people on Corps and Brigades staffs are being trained, that the lower units have suffered a bit. Some of the same held true for radio training as well, and no matter how we tried to excuse our plans, ultimately he was right. Otherwise, General Ali had nice things to say about what we are doing here in Gardez, and encouraged us to keep up the good work. After this short meeting, it was off to airport to drop off our VIP's, and as the airplane raised itself into the air, COL Rafi and I were able to finally able to exhale. Now back to our regularly scheduled business, now with a slightly adjusted focus on more training. I sure am glad that this sort of visit doesn't occur on a regular basis.

VIP's … Round Two. Talk about a lot to do in a short amount of time. Not but two days have passed since we sent General Ali back to

Kabul, and we have more VIP visitors headed our way. This time it was a couple of Generals, one from Poland and one from Turkey. To include we had some American bigwigs riding along with them. Their mission was to validate our newest training team from Poland. This being a multi-national effort, and all, we recently received a team of Polish mentors while I was away. They have spent the last couple of weeks training with our American mentors, to make sure that they are cool with the mission before them. They did swimmingly well, and now it was time for a ceremony to celebrate their accomplishments, and to also pass to them the banner of responsibility. First, before we could officially pass over responsibility, we they had to make sure they had the blessings of the two star General in charge of the whole mission here in Afghanistan. Now he didn't make the trip here himself, instead he stayed in Kabul, and we elected to talk to him via a video teleconference. Guess whose responsibility it is to make sure that this little chitchat can occur? That's right, you guessed it. Mine. No pressure, because the network works perfectly all the time here in Afghanistan, just like good old Ma Bell back home. After a couple days of preparation, we were ready for this, and I say we because my whole team had a hand in making this whole thing possible.

Everything went off without a hitch, well, there was one little hitch. No one noticed it, so I am not going to say anything about here. They know who they are, and what they did. After the approval from our two star General, it was time for the passing of the colors. This is a ceremony much like I explained on my blog a couple of postings ago. It is a symbolic passing of the units' colors from the old commander to the new commander. Great ceremony and all, and the best part was the new commanders speech, which took all of about two minutes. You have got to love that, and especially now that the days are starting to heat up around here. The mission here has been pretty cool, because I have been able to work with the ANA. Meeting new people, and learning about their culture, have been the coolest part of this mission. Not only have I been able to work with, and learn about the Afghans, but also I can add to that list the Romanians, Canadians, and our newest friends, the Polish. Sweet. Not to name drop, but the picture at the right is me, and a one star Turkish General from ISAF forces, just added another star to my constellation of stars throughout this blog.

Well … that's about all I want to say about Afghanistan. Just for those of you who have been curious about the amount of steak days left? Here's a shocker, six, that's right six. Six steak days left, and we'll be headed back to the USofA. If there are any people reading this that have influence on the whole extension thing, please don't, it would be so un-cool of you. I am so sick of steak. Be cool all, and I look forward to seeing you all so soon.   To the Kiwanis, thank you for your efforts in bringing much needed school supplies to the children of Afghanistan. Also, thank you all for the nice birthday and Easter wishes, they were all appreciated very much.

Until Next Time,
Mark

Talking Dirty Laundry, Indeed

"After enlightenment, the laundry."   *Zen Proverb*

Welcome back everyone. I am sitting here in my room on a Friday morning, or what I refer to as my cell, and am contemplating going back to sleep. Friday is what we call low op-tempo day, which stands for "low operations tempo." Friday is the religious day for Muslims, kind of like our Sunday, so most of our ANA counterparts go home for a day or two, and hang out with their families. This leaves us a day without mentoring, so it provides us time to do laundry, catch up with other work, or just do nothing. Don't tell my boss about that last one though, as we are not supposed to just do nothing. He'll say; "it's LOW op-tempo day, not NO op-tempo day," so we'll keep that last little nugget to ourselves. Over the last several days we have been working pretty hard on planning missions to thwart the efforts of the bad guys. As I am sure you are reading in the papers, or seeing on the television news, the bad dudes feel this spring needs to be their time to make a statement. Our plan is to simply not allow them to speak. However planning meetings that span from one day to the next, and then start again as the sun is rising, definitely takes it toll. It's kind of funny to see us all running around like zombies the last few days,

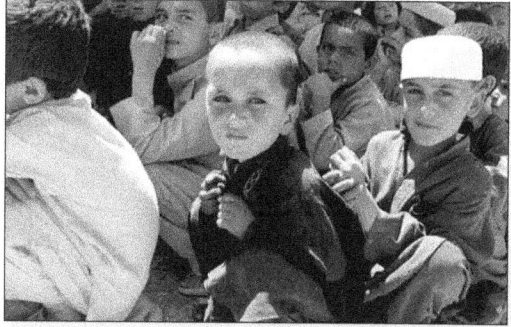

trying to keep up with the pace. It is a much needed pace, however, as we cannot let the dushman, Dari for enemy, get the best of the Afghan Army and Police.

Whew, that was awesome, just woke up from a forty-five minute nap. It was quite nice. Now, where were we? Oh yeah, since we have taken over training the police, as well as the Afghan Army, we have gotten everyone together for much better coordinated efforts against the dushman. Training the police was a mission well over due, and they certainly need the help. The Afghan Army, on the other hand, has had the assistance of   the American Army for a few years now, and I honestly think they are on the cusp of being independent. We have made a lot of progress with them, and they have done a lot of improvement on their own as well. So, focus on the police is happening at the right time, and the teams training them are already seeing results. It is kind of sad, but because of the lack of training the police currently have, they have become an easy target. However, speaking of results, they are learning. Here's a cool little story of two police heroes. There were a couple of ANP, Afghan National Police, guarding a training center entrance. Along comes what they believed to be suspicious motorcycle driver, trying to get close to the gate. They recognized that something was odd with the particular driver, so they decided to take a defensive stance, and

even chased the guy a bit, trying to figure out what the deal was. The motorcyclist, who happened to be strapped with explosives, was bent on blowing something up. Seeing that the cops were not going to let him make them martyrs, he immediately turned his bike around, and blew himself up to avoid capture. Thankfully, making himself the only martyr that day. The police dudes were given gifts from the police chief and certificates documenting their good day. Certificates of accomplishment are huge in this country. If you give someone a certificate for doing a good job, for them, it is better than gold.

Ohh … Be right back, got to throw my laundry in the washer. Doing laundry around here is quite an experience. As the camp fills up with more and more people moving in, it is getting a little more difficult to get laundry done. First off, we can't start laundry until eight in the morning, this allows for people in the showers to get adequate water pressure, and avoid being scalded. Once the morning's eighth hour hits, it's a free-for-all on the washers, like horses breaking out of the starting gates. Then once you have started your laundry, you never know where it is in the process it is, so it becomes a guessing game to find it at any one point. You see, the washers and dryers are in the restroom; hence it can be a little socially awkward to sit in there while your laundry is going through its cycles. So you load up a washer, or dryer, and trust that the laundry will be okay while you are away. When you think it is time to move your laundry from a washer to a dryer, which may have already been done by another anxious individual who needs the washer. Timing becomes everything in the laundry game. If you miss the exact moment your laundry is done in the washer, then you have to search all the dryers, trying to find out where your stuff ended up. Once located, then in go the dryer sheets, and again out of the restroom, so you can avoid the oddity of sitting in there. If you miss the time when your dryer is done, then hopefully your laundry is sitting atop the dryer, and everything is there. I am pretty sure this is the time where most of my missing socks wander off, I can't prove anything yet, but I am on the case.

OK, laundry is started, now where were we? If I haven't been involved in marathon planning meeting, I have been finding myself on the road a lot. In the last week I have driven the group commander, General Pritt and his replacement General Livingston, all over our chunk of Afghanistan. The new General is trying to get a feel for the lay of the land, and General Pritt is saying his goodbyes. When I haven't been driving around VIP's, I have found myself driving to Kabul and back, slowly but surely

getting our replacements down here. We are in the process of moving our whole group out of this country, and a new group is finding their way here. It is called a RIP or replacements in place. Because we so shorthanded with the guys that have already gone home, I chip in, and lend a hand at driving or gunning back and forth to get people moved where they need to be. Soon it will be our turn to leave this country, a measly twenty-three days to be exact. I can't wait, it certainly has been a long year here, and since I have been back from leave, some of the days have certainly dragged on. I am sure it is because I know I am so close to home now. It is cheerless to see some of my friends head home, and I will certainly miss them, but I also know I am not too far behind. It was someone's brainchild to send all the Afghan Army Trainers, ETT's, home on the last group leaving. Whoever this person is, I am definitely not his/her biggest fan, but reluctantly it makes sense and I agree with it. The reason is because we need to spend the most time we can with our replacements, make sure that the transfer between us and them goes as smoothly as possible. I received my first attempt at a replacement, but the guy that was sent to replace me is not really ready to take the reins of a Corps communications section, and he certainly didn't grasp the concept of mentoring. So, we are currently in search of another signal mentor, hopefully we find one soon. If anyone out there knows of anyone who can run a signal section, and mentor the ANA, please have them apply within. We are an equal opportunity employer.

Hold on, I'll be right back; it's time to go back to the laundry game, and make sure my stuff makes it into a dryer. That and I have to put in my three dryer sheets. I know, three seems excessive, but if I do not put three of them in there, then all my stuff will come out of the dryer in one giant static ball. I don't know what it is about this place, other than the air is incredibly dry, but static electricity is a huge problem, and I hate getting shocked all the damn time. Then I am going to run off to lunch. By the way here's a grilled cheese and tomato soup update. It hasn't happened again since that one day. I knew it was too good to be true. Now there's another thing I can't wait to leave behind. Not getting to choose what I am going to eat, or at least having a hand in preparing it. It is to the point where I can tell you what day it is simply by looking at what is being served at the chow hall. That's not good. I can't wait to cook something that I desire to eat, or choose off of a menu. The one saving grace of our chow hall is that they always have a decent variety of fresh fruits and vegetables, and I do appreciate that. That and I certainly do not want to complain about our accommodations here in Gardez, there are units even further down range who have it a lot worse off than we do. Anyways, be right back.

OK, lunch has been tolerated, now where were we? Oh yeah, I almost forgot to tell you the best thing I have done since we last spoke. We opened a new school a couple of days ago, in a place called Nik Nam. It was awesome. In addition, we also

delivered a ton of new school supplies to get the school started. The cool thing was that it was not only the US and the ANA participating with opening the school, but the ANP were also there to dedicate the school. To include, there were some local dignitaries, and someone from the Ministry of Education. It was a small, but pretty grand occasion. The school only had boys attending, so far; but hopefully it will soon have girls too. The reason for the lack of girls is that the school is located in one of the areas of Afghanistan that is not as progressive, so girls are not safe there. This particular school sits right across the street from a police outpost, so hopefully this will change in the near future. Other than that, I can't tell you a whole lot about the school opening this time, because I went as security this time, so during the festivities I didn't have much a view from my gun turret. As you can see from the picture at the end of this posting, my view was definitely spectacular, but sadly I could see much else. That's okay though, I do not want to hog the humanitarian missions. I want to make sure that everyone gets a chance to attend these events. Maybe if more people got involved in being a **human**itarian, we haven't to be here in the first place. The one thing I could see from

my perch atop the Humvee was the raising of the Afghan flag. That was a neat moment. It would be thoughtless of me if I didn't thank everyone back home for the continued support of our humanitarian efforts here.

Hold on, I'll be right back; it's time

to find out if I won the laundry game. Anytime I can get all clothes back in one bundle, static-cling free, and without socks missing. I can declare myself the winner. It's nice to be able to fold the clothes in my cell, and come up with everything I started with. Just think, I only have to do my laundry, maybe, three or four more times. Now there's a splendid thought. OK, be right back.

OK, laundry is fully accounted for, folded, and put away. Let it be officially noted, I am a winner of the laundry game today. Now where were we? Oh yeah, I think we were just wrapping things up here. I got everyone in the loop on the goings on around here, and what I have been up to lately, and why it as taken so long to write a new post.

Got a few people to make sure I thank before I wrap things up here. First of all, the Kiwanis, thank you for an incredible effort, and the children here will so appreciate all you have done. JJ and Carrie, thank you for all the stuff you sent, that was incredible. The catalogs and such went straight into our library when it got here, and I haven't seen them since, as they are always checked out. The other stuff went to our MWR, Morale Welfare and Recreation group, where they were given out as prizes for our poker tournaments. Let me tell you, people played just a bit harder to make it to the final table. Thank You, you guys rock. Angie and Agnieszka, thank you for your continued thoughts,

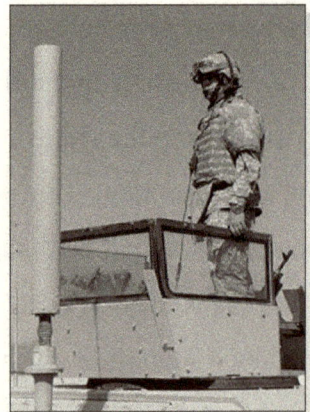

and boxes full of cool stuff. You are keeping our library, and our stomachs, full. Soon, because our time here is so short, I will be sitting down to write the overall year in perspective. I look forward to that endeavor. Talk to you all soon, and I am glad we could share this day together.

Sincerely,
Mark

Something Worth Leaving in Afghanistan: The Race Home

"History is a relentless master. It has no present, only the past rushing into the future." JFK

Welcome back everyone; as usual it is my hope that this posting reaches all of you in the best of health and spirits. We are ever so close to the end of this mission, and I am so anxiously, but patiently awaiting the end. I know my couch has been missing me desperately. This experience has been nothing but life altering, but as with all things, it too must come to an end. Recently my time has been spent just trying to wrap things up around here. I want to make sure that I leave my post as best I can, so the next guy can step in and make as seamless a transition as he can to his new post. I still have not received any news on a replacement, but do not worry, as it does not stop my leaving here. We have had tons of new soldiers moving to our area of the country as we slowly replace our rotation with theirs. This place is so overcrowded, as we make this transition, that we have people sleeping on cots in all kinds of strange places. Standing in line to get a meal, use the phones, or to use the washer and dryers, has now become the norm here. Thankfully, this is only a temporary predicament; soon a lot of the folks from our rotation will be making the move towards the USofA.

Ohh … the sounds of those words are like those Thin Mint cookies sold by the Girl Scouts. Awesome. As we are getting ready to move out, the season of a hundred and twenty days of wind have moved in. This place has been nothing but a giant wind tunnel, and I now know that I am a proven aerodynamic being. I could do without the dust storms though. These things are crazy, one second the sky is clear and beautiful, the next thing I know, I can't see the mountains anymore. The whole atmosphere is blanketed in a mass of dust and crap flying through the sky, I have never seen anything like it, and I don't remember it being that bad in Khowst last summer. Fortunately we

will not be here to see out the whole one hundred and twenty days. Hey, speaking of seeing the mountains around here. I know I talk about the views around here, and always try to explain just what the vistas here are like, I thought I would give you all a three hundred and sixty view of the place. If you click on the link below, you'll get to take a tour of our camp. You will need the QuickTime player to get it to work, which should be pretty simple. But once downloaded, simply left click and move your mouse cursor around the image, and it should move you throughout our chunk of Afghanistan. You can also use the plus and minus sign on the window to zoom in and out. You can either click the link below to view it in your browser, or you can right click it and do a "Save Target As", to keep a copy of it for yourself. Either way works, but if you open it in your browser, simply click the "Back" button to return to the Blog. Enjoy.

As I look at all the new soldiers moving in our area, I think back a bit, about a year to be exact. I bet I had the exact same look on my face as these guys do now. It's a look of not knowing exactly what to expect out of the deployment. The unknowing is the hardest part, and whenever I engage in a conversation with any of them, I try to tell them all I am familiar with, give them some sort of morsel of information that may be helpful. It's odd though, there's this fine line between being helpful, and sounding like the guy at the legion who starts all his stories with, "No shit … so there I was." I always make sure I am not that guy. Plus a lot of guys would rather have their stories unfold in front of themselves, without any sort of foreshadowing. Call it a male thing, or some sort of Army thing, but I usually do not start a conversation about my experiences here unless asked. The male psyche can be such an odd thing. Seeing all these new soldiers here is a good sensation though, because it is one more way to gauge just how close we are to getting out of here. I also like the enthusiasm the new guys are bringing with them. They all seem all fired up to get started with the mission, and continue where we left off. There are also a lot of the new guys here who will be embarking on the newest facet of our mission, and that is to train the Afghan Police. We kind of got it started, but as with anything new in the Army, it takes a little bit too really get things running. I think these guys have the energy to push it to the next level, and really get something going there that will help the police secure their cities and towns.

It has been a good year for me overall, and I feel pretty successful about what I have done here for the past year. I had been training in the National Guard for eighteen years, and it was positive for me to finally be able to put my training to work in a real life mission. But, even if I took all the Army stuff out of the mix, just on what we were able to do with our humanitarian efforts makes the year worth it. I think we made a heck of a difference here with the citizens, and if we were measuring success by thankful smiles, we would be off the charts. I wish we could have done more, but our mission didn't always allow for it. I also sometimes wish we could have done some other programs, like vocational training. It is great that we are able to help the people on the short term, but with something like vocational training, maybe we could also help them long term. I am sure that will be a consideration for the future. Right now, I would make the assumption that it is just not feasible with the security situation as it is. Just getting, and keeping, the children in school are challenging enough work.

As far as the Afghan Army is concerned, I think we made some headway towards putting this Army into a position where they can do

these things by themselves, which was our mission. I can't say we did this all by ourselves; they were pretty much on their way when we got here, but I think we helped with some fine tuning. Right now as we speak, the Afghan Army is planning a mission where they will take the entire lead. This is the first time that they will plan, prepare, practice, and then execute the mission with their Army as the lead element. They will, of course, have the support of us, but usually it is the other way around. This is a huge step for them, and I wish them all the luck. Sadly, we will not be here to see the results. Just the other day, during one of our mega-planning sessions, the Afghan Army took a field on the camp and turned it into a giant model depicting our mission. Once again, they had a little help on the model, but they moved their guys all over the model like giant chess pieces, depicting the movements they will execute during the mission. This is cool stuff to watch, although I am not a huge fan of the massive amount of time we spend sitting in meetings planning for this mission, but it is a necessary evil, to make sure all goes off without a hitch. This mission will be an enormous test for the Afghan Army, and I am sure there are a lot of people with much more rank than I, watching very intently over this whole thing. I am also sure that the ANA are aware of this, and they want to show everyone that they are a force to be reckoned with, and that they can do this stuff autonomously. I know people are going to want to know if my time here was worth the investment, and I am sure when I return, the question will come up quite a bit. It's a tough question, and I think I better come up with something before I get there. But, if I had to give the first instinctual answer my brain comes up with, then it is yes, we did do good things here. Maybe they are not articles that are immediately measurable, or they may not be bulleted objective

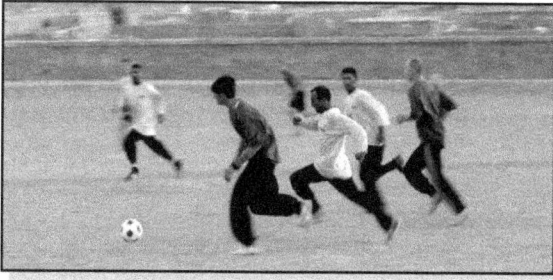

outcomes on some freaking Power Point slide that can pinpointed for some politician. Hopefully they are small thoughts within the intellect of the people of Afghanistan. That we are not here to change their Muslim beliefs, make them westerners like us, or that we want to open a Wal-Mart on every corner for that matter. That we are here to help them. Help them towards an Afghanistan that can stand on its own, and provide for its people safety and prosperity in a civilized fashion. Hopefully though just my interacting with the friends I have made here, that I have passed on these principles, and as they grow and develop, that they pass these ideals on. I will always keep Afghanistan, and all my Afghan friends, in my thoughts and prayers for a long time. I hope for progressively continued success for them, and for the soldiers who fall in behind me to continue the mission.

Whew ... Sorry about that didn't mean to get on my philosophical and political soapbox. Sometimes that happens. I guess I just want to make sure people know that this isn't all about removing the Taliban from Afghanistan. We can do that a million times over. It is about leaving the Afghans with the idea that they can do it, and trust me, sometimes it is a tough sell for a people who have been involved in some sort of a war for so many decades. Anyhow, check this out. We have been looking for ways to get more involved with the Afghan Army here on a more social level. Someone got the brainchild to challenge our Afghan brethren here to a soccer game, or it could have been the other way around, I am not sure. C'mon now, this is

Afghanistan, these guys are nutso for the soccer, and they will destroy us. Not only that, but this is their home court. They are used to the altitude and the fans

will totally be on their side. This was going to be tough. One of the Iowa guys here spent a ton of time putting together the contest, and to ensure we had a fighting chance, we enlisted the help of our coalition partners, the Polish, Romanians, and even a couple of Interpreters. If we were going to take on the mighty Afghan Army soccer team, we had to do everything we could. Call it stacking the deck if you will, we called it making sure that our coalition partners were involved in the fun, but deep down we wanted to win. Who doesn't? The cool Iowa guy even created a traveling trophy for the event. Why traveling? Well, we knew no matter who won the challenge, of course there would have to be a rematch. Neither team would let it rest at one win, or one loss for that matter. I am sure this will develop into some sort of recurring challenge. For our replacements, sorry about that, hope you like soccer. After much planning, preparation, and trophy building, the big day came along. The Afghan was a svelte athletic looking bunch; our team had quite a challenge ahead of them. Our team didn't look half bad themselves. Game on. It was a rousing contest, and if I were even remotely in soccer I may have been able to tell you what occurred, but the end result. Afghan Army scored one, and the Coalition team had two of the balls roll into the netted area, which means we won... I guess. Cool, but I am guessing that the rematch will have a better prepared or stacked, whichever way you go on that one, Afghan team than ours. Wish the next guys all the luck on that one.

Here is another example of progress in our area of operations. Our first big group of basic training soldiers has graduated from their training. It was a cool occasion, mostly for them, as they have officially become Afghan Army soldiers. The next step for them is moving on to the job specific training. We will be keeping a lot of the soldiers around here, because we have now opened a basic infantryman's course here. I remember how much trouble they were

having marching when they first started here. I was hard not to laugh, but I think it was not really they, but memories of me going

through the same thing almost twenty years ago. Now when they march around the camp, they are doing it synchronously. They also seem to hold their heads up just a bit higher than when they first got there. We are all so pumped up for them, and were so proud of the progress that they have made, so I thought I would show you all a few shots of them. This is the future of the Army. Good luck gentlemen.

Well, this is the saddest part of the posting. This is the part where I have to say good-bye. However, I will see you all sooner than you think. About nineteen days to be exact, give or take a day, so I guess I can't be all that exact. If I do the math, that's only two more steak days, two more showers, and two more clothes washing days. OK, only kidding about the shower thing. It's close though, and I am counting the days. I also want to make sure that I thank all the people who have supported me though this crazy year and a half. There really is no way to properly show my gratitude. All the packages I have received, humanitarian aid and morale wise, were all so appreciated. The letter and cards were always fun to read, and too so deeply appreciated. Everything was awesome, ad I couldn't have made it through all this time without them. I thank you from all that I am, and see you all soon. I believe I may owe some of you a libation or two, I'll see what I can do to remedy that when I return.

Sincerely,
Mark

Home . . . Now What

"Home is an invention on which no one has yet improved."   *Douglas*

Hello Everyone. Welcome back to the final installment of this blog. The Iowa team has been back home for two months now, and so it is time that I complete this. I must say that this has been one of the hardest parts of the deployment, the "How to end this record of my journey." I have thought about, and struggled with it for a long time, on how I can put into words what I experienced as we left Afghanistan. Well, here goes, and hopefully I am able to capture everything appropriately into words.   Getting out of the country wasn't as easy as we had hoped, and it seemed like it was never going to happen at times. Transportation out was certainly not an easy task, especially for the amount of people that were have trying to get out of there. There were a lot of time spans in which we simply sat around and waited until our ride showed up. Once the team got out of Gardez, and moved to Kabul, the waiting game definitely took hold. We were able to out-process of Kabul within a day or so, so that went pretty quick. Then the movement to the next station, Kuwait, took entirely way too much time. We spent a lot of our spare time drinking coffee at the Green Bean, the local java hangout at lovely Camp Phoenix. We also went to the PX numerous times. Although I really didn't have anything I wanted, or needed to buy, it was just something to help pass the time. The rest of the time was spent reading, watching the 'ol iPod, or sleeping in the tent. Finally the day came, our flight was confirmed, and we were off to Kuwait. Thank God. We loaded up our stuff, and ourselves in the back of giant trucks, for what would be our last convoy in Afghanistan. It was the best ride of my life. The choking dust, horrific smells, oppressive heat, and cramped space was the usual horrible, yet the ride was awesome. This was it, the last one, and after a few hours of waiting at the Kabul International Airport, we were in the air. Good Bye Afghanistan. Although I couldn't wait to get home, and back to my "normal" life, I still felt as if I were leaving something behind. Hard to believe that I could actually be saddened by the thought of leaving what was my home for just over a year, but it was true. I was sad for the soldiers, both US and Afghan that I was leaving. I have made some lifelong friends there, and leaving them was not easy. I am sure the thought of returning home, and trying to assimilate myself back into what was my life also nagged at me, somewhere in the back of my mind. How does one who has spent the last year of life go from living la vida loca to living la blando Iowa? The year was spent on edge, always being totally aware of everything, and now I will no longer have to do that. I don't have to worry about someone lobbing rockets at my home, or trying to blow up my car on the highway, or at least I hope not. But I knew that this metamorphosis had to take place, and I think the nagging part was the how it was to occur.

I am abruptly returned to reality when the C-17 aircraft we were flying in started its decent into Kuwait. I vaguely recall the flight, so it must not have been all that bad. What I do clearly remember is Kuwait is the hottest, windiest, and driest place on planet earth. As we stepped off the rear of the aircraft, and into what I am sure was indication as to what hell may be like, we were immediately shuffled onto air conditioned busses. Another Thank God moment on the journey home. Again, we were subject to several days of wait time, and everywhere you went had to be via movement outside in the windy heat. Uhhhggg, but at least in Kuwait we had a McDonalds, Pizza Hut, and KFC to eat, and huge movie rooms to hang out in, and other creature comforts that made the time pass by a bit quicker than it did in Kabul. The only thing that really sticks out in my brain about

Kuwait, besides the various camel spiders we encountered, was the customs process. Simply put, it sucked. I know it

has to be done, we certainly wouldn't want American soldiers to get caught trying to sneak their interpreters home, but seems to me we could do away with some of the crap they had us do. Well, we make it through the process, and now we are finally on our way back to the United States of America. After several hours in the air, a quick pit stop in Germany, and then several more hours in the air, we are over

America Air space. Of course the plane erupted with cheers, and the excitement level of everyone in the aircraft went up about ten notches, but we still have several hours to go. Our first stop back in the USofA was Colorado to drop some stuff off, and then we had to board a bus for several more hours of seat time for our bona fide destination. Fort Riley, Kansas, for one of several out processing episodes we have to endure. Once at Fort Riley, we were afforded an opportunity to catch up on our sleep by having to sit through two days of briefings. They were pretty much the same ones we received in Kabul, and I am sure to be the same ones we will have to sit through once we return to Iowa. Now don't get me wrong, the information given out in the briefings is important, and we should pay attention to what's being put out. But when all that is on your mind is being a couple of hours away from home, where my family and friends are, and the realization that the journey is finally coming to an end. It was just too hard to try and pay attention. I was doing all I could to hold myself back from running to the nearest Hertz, renting myself a car, and heading back to Iowa. I don't think that would have gone over to well at all, but it was tempting. Now the final ride home. The last day spent at Fort Riley was short; we all loaded up on a bus for the last leg of our voyage early that Fathers Day morning, off to Newton, Iowa. What a Fathers Day to remember. I don't think that freaking bus could have gone fast enough, and the energy on that machine was nuts. There were signs posted along the highway as we neared our destination, and we even got an escort from some cops and Harley riders. It was an interesting mixture of fellows that shepherded us in, but none the less, it was a great American sight. Finally arriving in Newton, God, and the emotions that welled in me is indescribable. Once lined up, we marched into the High School gymnasium, and made a line across the floor. On display for everyone to see, their heroes were home, at last. I saw my family right away, and once again, inexpressible. There were a couple of people that wanted to publicly thank us, and that's cool, but I really didn't hear a word they said. No disrespect, but they were just not at the front of priority list. Thankfully, they understood that, and kept their comments quite short. Then we were released to our families. I lost sight of everything, and everyone else, and sought my family out. We hugged and kissed, and in between answered questions from reporters, extended family, and friends. It was one of the most awesome moments of my life. Oddly, the second I was with my family, all the time that was lost due to the separation immediately melted away. It didn't seem as if we were gone at all, like I was able to shed that layer of skin right off. The brain is such a wonderful organ, having the ability to bring me right back to where I was before I

left, so I thank you memory. We loaded up the car with the stuff I had, said some quick goodbyes, and we were off to an unknown destination.

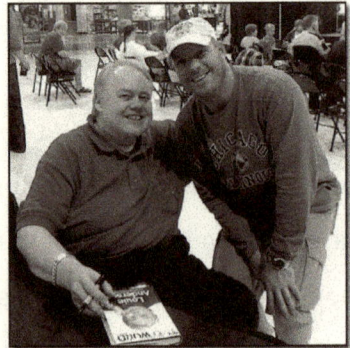

Since that day I have since returned to work, and an almost normal life again, so that's cool. And, of course, I have the memories of one of the greatest vacations of my life. Now off to my next adventure, and who knows what it will be. I certainly want to make sure that I thank everyone, who contributed in every facet possible, to make the vacation a success. I appreciate the support of my family and friends, for without them, this journey would have been pretty empty. Lastly, let me thank whatever Supreme Being there may be for allowing me to remain unharmed while away, there were a lot of my brethren who were not as fortunate, and may that same divinity smile down upon them.

Signing Off,
Mark

Acknowledgements

I have to first and foremost thank my family, if it were not for them; this journey would not have been as significant. Especially to my wife, Shelly, who during the entire process was as solid as a rock, and thanks for pushing me to get this done as well.

I have to thank the Iowa National Guard for presenting me with the opportunity to take this trip, and for supporting the team throughout the process. The same goes towards the South Dakota National Guard, who sent an amazing team to live and work with. To further, damn near every states' ETT team was an absolute joy to work with, they were completely professional, and I wish all of those soldiers the best as they are returned to their homes with their families.

Although I mention them all quite a bit throughout the blog, I would be amiss if I didn't mention them here, and that was all the people who donated supplies to both the soldiers and to our humanitarian efforts. It was these people who provided us an opportunity to not only do our jobs in Afghanistan, but they provided us the means to help the citizens of Afghanistan. To make a difference in the lives of the people who are living a daily struggle of survival during incredibly hard times. May they one day appreciate the beauty of peace.

www.ingramcontent.com/pod-product-compliance
Lightning Source LLC
Chambersburg PA
CBHW031841090426
42741CB00005B/318